KU-705-102

PRIMARY SCIENCE
Making it Work

The book is dedicated to

Dave, Nicholas, Christopher, Debbie and Kait

Jill, Anna, Kate and Lucy.

PRIMARY SCIENCE
Making it Work

Chris Ollerenshaw
and
Ron Ritchie

David Fulton Publishers
London

David Fulton Publishers Ltd
2 Barbon Close, London WC1N 3JX

First published in Great Britain by
David Fulton Publishers 1993

Note: The right of the authors to be identified as the authors of this work has
been asserted by them in accordance with the Copyright, Designs and Patents
Act 1988.

Copyright © Chris Ollerenshaw and Ron Ritchie

British Library Cataloguing in Publication Data

A catalogue record for this book is available from the British Library

ISBN 1–85346–199–7

All rights reserved. No part of this publication may be reproduced, stored in a
retrieval system or transmitted, in any form, or by any means, electronic,
mechanical, photocopying, recording or otherwise, without the prior
permission of the publishers.

Typeset by Action Typesetting Limited, Gloucester
Printed in Great Britain by BPCC Wheatons Ltd, Exeter

Contents

The Primary Science Case-studies

Preface

The following chapters are the result of collaboration between the authors over a number of years, initially as advisory teachers and, later, in institutes of higher education. Our lengthy association has involved working with, and alongside, primary teachers in diverse circumstances. We recognise that our experience, from our class-teacher beginnings to the writing of this book, has been an active and creative process. No-one has transplanted understanding into our heads, nor have we reached it down, ready-made, from a shelf. Indebted as we are to our enablers, and especially to those who were responsible for the central, revelatory, research (duly credited elsewhere and mentioned here with thanks), we have, nevertheless, constructed our own understanding of the nature of learning in science and of teaching strategies that can best enable it. This is, in point of fact, the constructivist view of learning and it is this view which forms the basis of the book. And in keeping with this constructivist view we add the rider that the substance of our thesis represents only our current best explanations in response to a complex series of questions about the nature of learning and teaching.

The case-studies we quote from have been collected over several years from teachers with whom we have had direct contact and are they part of our evidence that teachers can adopt a constructivist approach in the classroom and make it work. We hope that you, the reader, will make use of the text and case studies and that they will enable you to clarify, and perhaps modify, your existing ideas about learning and teaching in science. The teachers' comments, and our own analysis of these classroom episodes, are offered to focus your attention upon what actually happens when children engage in scientific activities, and on the role of the teacher in facilitating their learning. If we have been successful, these glimpses into classrooms will stimulate you to collect evidence from your own teaching in order to identify and evaluate ways in which children's learning can be better promoted. The most significant contribution to your understanding will come from this kind of reflection upon your own classroom experience and from your enquiries into different aspects of your practice.

There are three inextricably linked themes running through the book which can be related to children's learning and teachers' professional development. The first relates to active engagement in a process: for children, the process involves exploration and investigation of the world around them; for the teacher it is a process of engaging with the text, the case studies, and school children directly, to reflect upon current practice and to explore new approaches to teaching. The second theme concerns the active construction of tentative understanding: for children this relates to their construction of scientific ideas; for the teacher, it involves constructing an understanding of how children learn and how the teaching affects that learning. The third theme relates to the social context in which learning, for child and teacher, takes place. There is a tendency to see learning as individualistic, and in some respects this is appropriate since we all construct a unique understanding. However, learning is constantly affected by social factors. Much learning for children in science occurs in group situations and talk is as important to learning in science as doing. For teachers, too, we emphasise the importance of collaboration with colleagues and of the social context in which teaching occurs.

Acknowledgements

We would like to acknowledge the contribution of all the teachers whose work is included in this book and of those who have helped us, through sharing their classroom experiences and ideas, to construct our present understanding.

Finally, but not least, our thanks go to those close to us for their tolerance, support and encouragement. We are grateful to Dave for continuous checking and correction of texts, to Jill for proofreading, and to Nicholas for indefatigable word-processing.

CHAPTER 1

Introduction

1. The beginning.

This book is intended to be a practical working guide to the teaching of science. We hope it will be of use to both the established primary class-teacher and the student. It is an account of a particular approach to teaching which combines workable classroom practice with current understanding of the way children learn. The underlying view is learning-centred and holistic. This approach has already received extensive trialling and is being increasingly adopted in primary schools. The outcomes to date have been highly encouraging. We are also confident we can provide realistic advice and reassurance for teachers who did not specialise in science and who may be worried about their own lack of recent experience in Science National Curriculum territory.

Let us begin on the big easel:

> The world is in revolution. Technology is rampant. Whole economies are dependent on science and its applications. The human organism is reaching inwards, as well as outwards, towards the very determinants of Life itself. Centres of power lie within high-security areas, accessed by permit. The public catches only glimpses, through barbed wire, of vague super-beings moving like shadows through blinding light.

The above paragraph parodies a nineteen fifties' science-fiction scenario for the future ... yet already, all of it has a parallel in the real world.

It has been apparent for some considerable time now that the future of the world lies in the hands of scientists and technologists as much as in those of politicians. It is not surprising, therefore, that in due course, the traditional credo of education gave way to new thinking. Our children were given the Science National Curriculum (DES, 1992a). And the question arose – who was there to teach it in primary schools? Who indeed? How can a non-specialist teach science in the detail demanded?

Fortunately, the teaching of primary science, although it does obviously involve content, is equally about establishing attitudes and working practices which will first catch and then nurture, the germinal concepts of children. Most primary teachers will by now have been comforted by the knowledge that they are not expected to condense complex theory into child language. If any remain who haven't, we will say right away, that primary science should not be a watered-down version of secondary science. The kind of science teaching advocated in this book aims at giving children a clear understanding of basic concepts. We say 'giving' in the interests of a crisp style. In point of fact, 'enabling the children to acquire', expresses our philosophy better, but is less gripping. This longer phrase also suffers from an intrinsic vagueness of the kind which besets discovery learning and which invites method-abuse. What we offer is anything but vague. Children taught as we suggest tend to become more specific, more alert, meticulous, laterally thinking and persevering. At all events, the clearer understanding of basic science concepts and the process skills which gradually emerge with it, will provide, we believe, the necessary hooks on which later, more theoretical, learning can be hung. The overall aim is to enfranchise the public at large. The parody at the beginning of the chapter was not just an illustration of the speed of change, it was a sad allegory of the position in which many people find themselves – debarred from lucrative and interesting pursuits and careers, basically through lack of expertise. They have no permits. Too many view science as outsiders. If more people can be enabled to handle science at secondary level or beyond, with less difficulty than before and to have an informed voice in the new society, then developments in primary science teaching will have been well worth the effort. We are attempting to create a more science-literate community. It is time everyone had a pass.

And now to the matter at hand.

2. What is Science?

Science is an exploration of the cosmos in order to discover or explain what, why, when, where and how things happened, are happening or are likely to happen within it. We are back to the big easel and a lot of it is out of reach. Scientists have to put forward theories and develop 'models' to help explain phenomena and to communicate their ideas to others. Their theories do not amount to an unchanging body of knowledge. At any given moment all one can say is that they form a currently accepted view of phenomena that helps us all to understand better what we find in the universe and on our own planet. It is also possible for scientists to hold differing theories about the same evidence. Science advances by the testing of theories and predictions in order to gain new evidence. This, in turn, may confirm hypotheses for the moment or refute them, or it may reveal new phenomena.

Science is therefore concerned with two things:

i.   Investigative processes;
ii. Current scientific theories.

'Science in the National Curriculum' stresses the equal importance of these two aspects of science. 1. Investigative Processes, is represented in Attainment Target 1 (A.T. 1). 2. Current Scientific Theories, is represented in A.T.s 2, 3 and 4 together. These cover: Life and Living processes; Materials and their properties; Physical processes.

3. What do Scientists Do?

In their search for understanding scientists do many things, including observing, checking, recording, thinking, reading, comparing their own ideas with those of other scientists, asking questions, testing hypotheses, carrying out investigations and collecting evidence.

The work of science demands that the individuals involved develop a respect for evidence – good science is not about good guesswork, it is about the imaginative cross-referencing of clues, the elimination of irrelevancies and the use of evidence to explain events. Again, scientists have good reasons for what they do: they do not work in the dark when they investigate. Sometimes discoveries are made but they are rarely accidental. Most often, discoveries arise from investigations which have been carefully structured. Science in the primary school can mirror these processes and activities. Children can explore and learn through observing, explaining, predicting, reading, talking, testing ideas, questioning, and planning further investigations. As with scientists, children will develop a systematic way of working and respect for evidence.

4. Constructivism and a constructivist approach to teaching science

What is constructivism?

Constructivism is a perception of the way learning takes place. It views individuals as active constructors of understanding. It suggests that people make their own interpretations of the information received through their senses. The resultant ideas and concepts may or may not be similar to those of other individuals. People carry portmanteaux of self-made working concepts through their lives and use them to interpret daily experiences. Information which does not fit these concepts is likely to be rejected or to go unnoticed. Only when the issue is forced, usually by ensuing misfortune, will a concept be re-evaluated and modified. Such modification is traditionally termed 'learning by experience' or, if something unpleasant results, 'learning the hard way'. Constructivism makes the point that the abandoning of the redundant concept, or the modification of it in the light of the new experience, is still a creative reaction which only the owner of the concept can effect.

Scott (1987) summarises Driver and Bell (1985) as follows:

> A constructivist view of learning
> 1. Learning outcomes depend not only on the learning environment but also on the prior knowledge, attitudes and goals of the learner.
> **What is already in the learner's mind matters.**
> 2. Learning involves the construction of knowledge through experience with the physical environment and through social interaction
> **Individuals construct their own meaning.**

3. Constructing links with prior knowledge is an active process involving the generation, checking and restructuring of ideas and hypotheses.
    The construction of meaning is a continuous and active process.
4. Learning science is not simply a matter of adding to and extending existing concepts, but may involve their radical re-organisation.
    Learning may involve conceptual change.
5. Meanings, once constructed, can be accepted or rejected.
    The construction of meaning does not always lead to belief.
6. Learning is not passive. Individuals are purposive beings who set their own goals and control their own learning.
    Learners have the final responsibility for their learning.
7. Students frequently bring similar ideas, about natural phenomena, to the classroom. This is hardly surprising when one considers the extent of their shared experiences – school life, hobbies, clubs, television, magazines, music etc.
    Some constructed meanings are shared.

The classroom is a highly controlled environment in which life's experiences can be simulated in different ways according to need – which is a good thing because we need to ensure children will want to reorganise or replace their redundant concepts without misfortune or unpleasantness as the spur. One thing is certain – that every child will arrive with a bag of concepts and ideas which will, to a large extent, affect subsequent learning. As teachers we have to bring child and experience together and then, with the aid of our professional expertise, ensure interaction between the two which will result in redundant concepts being modified or replaced in the light of the experience. We can manipulate the experiences in order to confront chosen concept areas but in every case the child's existing ideas and understanding are the clay and the child the sculptor. The teacher is the enabler, the catalyst, the mirror, the challenger.

Much work on a constructivist approach to children's learning in science has been undertaken, primarily in secondary schools, (The Childrens Learning in Science Project: CLIS, 1984-91) and has since been developed to illuminate frameworks for planning and developing work in the primary school (Science Processes and Concept Exploration Project, 1990, and Practical Issues in Primary Education No.6, 1990). Our own variant, taken from the

INSET materials produced as a result of a project on assessment in science, sponsored by Avon LEA via the N.P.C., in which we were involved, is as follows:

A CONSTRUCTIVIST VIEW OF LEARNING

ORIENTATION
Arousing children's interest and curiosity
ELICITATION/STRUCTURING
Helping children to find out and clarify what they think
INTERVENTION/RESTRUCTURING
Encouraging children to test their ideas:
to extend, develop or replace them
REVIEW
Helping children to recognise the significance
of what they have found out
APPLICATION
Helping children to relate what they have learned
to their everyday lives.

(Ollerenshaw et al., 1991)

Our approach to teaching is based on this model. Anyone coming to it for the first time has to recognise these essential characteristics:

(i) The process begins with what children already know, understand and can do. This means work for the teacher as much of it has to be excavated.

(ii) Children become the constructors of their own knowledge – with the guidance of the teacher. The onus for decision-making passes to the child. The teacher does not provide 'right' answers nor suggest directly how appropriate solutions might be found.

(iii) Child-to-child communication, especially in speech, is a necessary ingredient. Child-language is acceptable throughout. Universal terms are introduced at the end of events if it is appropriate to do so.

(iv) The focal point of the whole learning environment is each separate, individual, child – albeit in group contexts.

(v) Teaching is a process of enabling. It comprises ceaseless assessment of all children, individually, and appropriate actioned responses. These responses, apart from provisioning and recording, are for the most part in the form of verbal questions to help children clarify their thinking, to elicit where children's understanding has reached or to challenge children to think and act more carefully.

It is important to make a distinction between the constructivist approach and 'Discovery' learning. Discovery learning is based on the premise that if children are presented with the right materials and asked open-ended questions they will learn by discovering for themselves the concepts which lie in wait. The constructivist approach does not eschew discovery, rather it recognises its value as one of a wide range of learning situations. Constructivists are not limited to one method of application. Practitioners are free to use different teaching devices provided they are governed by the model of learning and the requirements described earlier as 'characteristics'.

The advantages of the constructivist approach to science in the primary classroom include the bringing together of what we know to be the value of investigative work with what we know of the way knowledge and understanding develop so that learning becomes a natural and logical process akin to established scientific procedures. As the process component itself is structured and disciplined through work in the classroom, children soon pick up the associated skills and are thereby enabled to pursue their own initiatives. What at first introduction might seem to the teacher to be an impossibly comprehensive mix of teaching objectives is soon resolved to manageable proportions as the children lose their teacher-dependency. There is also a marked improvement in individual children's behaviour. Children with apparent behavioural or social problems have frequently been shown, in practice, to perform well in these circumstances.

It is as if the provision of tools, the freedom to use them and the respect inherent in a teacher's invitation to use initiative reduces the need to challenge the imposed order of the classroom. Another factor is that the regular dialogue with the teacher, where the teacher is demonstrably interested in what the child thinks as something to value instead of something to be compared with a notionally 'correct' answer, has an elevating effect on the child's self-esteem. It can be a revelation to children who, as early as six or seven years of age, may already be associating themselves with failure.

It should be remembered, however, that these observations hold true only if the science activities are seen to be purposeful and where carelessness and inappropriate thinking are challenged by the teacher. Allowing a child to think almost anything will do is method abuse. Such abuse will produce more behaviourial problems, not fewer. This principle is so fundamental it will appear in different guises throughout the book.

On pages 10 and 11 the constructivist model is tabled along with details of the method which relates to it. You will notice that in our approach we have divided the model's five basic components into three. The first is 'exploration', which comprises the model's 'orientation' and 'elicitation'. Both these are fairly informal elements and have the feel of an exploration. The second is 'investigation' which comprises 'intervention / restructuring' and 'review', and reflects the formal and purposeful nature of the two model elements. Lastly there is 'application', based on the model element of the same name.

It should be remembered that the whole of the model of learning is exhausted in a minute if that is how long a child takes to learn something. It can take a week or longer to run through if complex subject matter is being dealt with. This longer version of the model is itself made up of short learning events – each of which can involve the whole model. In the teaching strategy under discussion we allocate quite long periods of activity to each of the steps in the model simply because the subject matter is usually complex and because we have to ensure that a number of children have reasonable doing, thinking and talking time at each stage. The real-life learning process of individual children varies enormously. The danger of publishing models like the one above is that they are compartmentalised whereas the ways individuals engage in these processes are not. We need the compartments in the way we need stereotypes – to begin to make sense of extremely complex material.

For science to be managed in the way we suggest there are implications for the role of the teacher and for the selection of materials and activities. The teacher's role varies over the whole process from the early orientation stage to the later application stage. This role starts by being unobtrusive, moves to being gradually more interventionist, then goes back to a non-interventionist role before becoming, finally, that of consultant, during a sequence of related activities. Such a role reflects a theory of teaching as 'assisted performance' discussed by R. Tharp and R. Gallimore (1991). They claim that:

> The lifelong learning by any individual is made up of the same, ZPD[1] sequences – from other-assistance to self-assistance – recurring over and over again for the development of new capacities.' (Light, Sheldon and Woodhead, 1991: 54)

The teacher's responsibility is to adjust to the differing demands of the 'buds' and 'flowers' of development. Recognising the development of children's thinking requires an observant teacher at all times but is made manageable by structuring and operating activities with this in mind.

The activities selected must support each particular element in the learning process. The type and function of activities will vary: some will be very practical, some based on discussion and some on reading. Activities may be the related to functions of an individual child, small groups of children (two or three), larger groups of children (four to six) or a whole class.

The teacher's role and the function of selected activities within the constructivist model are summarised on pages 12 and 13.

These themes will be returned to throughout the book and in greater detail.

5. Planning for Science

Planning for constructivist science teaching is an all-pervading skeletal structure, rather like coral. Whereas traditional teaching techniques can be serviced by planning on a weekly basis within an overall framework, the constructivist approach cannot. Its child-centred nature presents particular problems. Children

---

[1]ZPD: The Zone of Proximal Development Vygotskian theory (1978: 86) summarised by Tharp and Gallimore: 'The zone of proximal development defines those functions that have not yet matured but are in the process of maturation, functions that will mature tomorrow but are currently in an embryonic state.These functions could be termed the 'buds' or 'flowers' of development rather than the 'fruits' of development.' (Light, Sheldon and Woodhead, 1991: 45)

DEVELOPING CHILDREN'S OWN IDEAS ...
Teaching science begins with finding out what children think ...

EXPLORATION Abstracting general ideas from a range of specific experiences or from information gained from secondary sources	**ORIENTATION** Arousing children's interest and curiosity	Children focus their thinking informally on a defined subject area; the nature of this definition may itself help children to organise their knowledge in new ways, i.e. 'living and non-living things', 'what things are made of and why', 'what makes things move', etc.
	ELICITATION/ STRUCTURING Helping children to find out and clarify what they think.	Children are helped to discover what they already know; to become aware of what they think and why. They are encouraged to recognise that other people may have different ideas and to question why they have come to hold them, e.g. 'I think light things float, you think it's to do with what they are made of and she thinks things only float if they have got air in.'
INVESTIGATION Devising specific investigations to check the validity or usefulness of general ideas or hypotheses	**INTERVENTION/ RESTRUCTURING** Encouraging children to test their ideas: To extend, develop or replace them.	Children begin to compare alternative ideas in a systematic way, guided and supported by the teacher but always working from their own understanding, so that they are able to recognise results or outcomes that do not correspond to the idea being investigated, even if it is their own. Demonstration experiments which seem overwhelmingly convincing to the teacher may leave children unimpressed if they have not understood the thinking behind them.
	REVIEW Helping children to recognise the significance of what they have found out.	Having planned and carried out a systematic test children need to go beyond merely reporting their results. They need to be helped to identify what conclusions can be drawn from the information they have collected, e.g.: - Was their test fair or have new factors emerged that were not allowed for when it was planned? - Do they need to carry out any further tests? - Do their results support or challenge the hypothesis being tested?
APPLICATION Identifying specific applications for general ideas.	**APPLICATION** Helping children to relate what they have learned to their everyday lives.	After subjecting a variety of ideas to systematic testing and having decided which, if any, are worth retaining, children need opportunities to find out how these ideas can help to explain 'real-life' situations and how they can help to solve real problems. This stage of the development of understanding is particularly important because if children do not have opportunities to relate their learning to their own experience they are unlikely either to value or to remember new ideas.

... THROUGH THE PROCESS OF SCIENTIFIC ENQUIRY
... so that activities can be planned to build on their understanding

OBTAINING INFORMATION	Observing	- Deciding what to focus on, what is significant.
	Using secondary sources	- Referring to secondary sources, books, poster etc.
	Discussing	- Discussing relevant experiences with others.
ORGANISING INFORMATION	Classifying	- Comparing, sorting and ordering.
	Discussing/reporting	- Relating new information to what is already known.
	Recording	- Recording, collating and presenting information.
	Explaining	- Speculating on possible explanations.
	Finding patterns	- Looking for patterns, regularities, causes/effects.
	Predicting/Hypothesising	- Suggesting 'rules' or principles.
RAISING QUESTIONS	Predicting/Hypothesising	- 'Wondering' about the implications of rules/patterns.
	Raising questions	- Suggesting further lines of enquiry.
PLANNING TESTS	Discussing	- Clarifying exactly what is to be investigated - why?
	Identifying and controlling variables.	- Deciding what needs to be kept the same, what will be changed and how the effect will be observed/measured.
	Estimating	- Considering the likely range of results.
CARRYING OUT TESTS	Following written instructions	- (Only if the teacher can be sure that the purpose of the activity will be understood).
	Controlling variables	- Ensuring factors not being tested are kept constant.
	Observing	- Paying careful attention to effects of any changes.
	Measuring	- Quantifying results, choosing appropriate units/tools.
	Recording/Note-taking	- Deciding what needs to be recorded/how to present it.
	Considering safety	- Showing awareness of possible dangers, glass/heat etc.
REVIEWING RESULTS	Identifying variables	- Recognising factors not considered in planning.
	Explaining/Interpreting	- Considering the implications of results/findings.
	Drawing conclusions	- Referring back: is hypothesis supported/challenged?
	Discussing/Reporting	- Deciding, with others, what has been found out.
	Recording	- Choosing the clearest way to present findings.
	Hypothesising	- Developing or modifying earlier hypotheses.
RECOGNISING APPLICATIONS	Drawing on relevant experience	- Recognising events or situations from one's own experience which a new idea may help to explain.
	Identifying needs	- Finding contexts in which newly developed ideas and opportunities could help to solve problems.
PROBLEM SOLVING	All of the skills listed above	- Being able to apply newly acquired understanding in the process of investigating new problems.
	Generating a design	- Planning projects which draw on new understanding.
	Planning and making	- Using new ideas without prompting from teacher.

12

THE TEACHER'S ROLE:

The teacher has to be an enabler, not only helping children during their activities, but
planning the topic, organising the classroom, making materials available and establishing
a climate in which children are free to discuss and explore their ideas. Through sensitive questioning,
setting the children an example of how to use process skills, displaying positive attitudes towards science
and giving children support when and where they need it, the teacher will be promoting effective learning in science.

ORIENTATION
- Choose a 'Big Idea' (Chapter 2) to focus on, i.e. 'Forms of energy',
  'Properties of materials', 'Why living things are as they are'.
- Plan an initial stimulus to arouse children's interest and curiosity.
- Give children time to familiarise themselves with materials related
  to the chosen 'Big Idea'.
- Give children time to think and time to discuss and organise their ideas.

ELICITATION/
STRUCTURING
- Help the children to become clear about what they think and to
  develop their ideas.
- Offer opportunities for them to explore all ideas, not just their own.
- Question the children in a sensitive and appropriate way.
- Consider ways of building on the understanding revealed in explor-
  atory activities.
- Give them time to listen to and time to discuss each other's ideas.
- Select significant or revealing actions or comments to record as part
  of an assessment of their skills and understanding.
- Help them to develop their process skills.
- Emphasise that what children think is as important as what they know.

INTERVENTION/
RESTRUCTURING
- Provide opportunities for systematic testing.
- Help the children extend, develop or replace their ideas.
- Help the children develop their process skills by setting an example
  and by questioning appropriately.
- Record significant examples of children's use of process skills.
- Provide opportunities for children to discuss each other's ideas.
- Challenge children's ideas and suggest alternatives for consideration
  and testing.

REVIEW
- Offer opportunities for discussion between you and the child and
  between children, referring back to their previous ideas.
- Help the children see the significance of what they have found out.

APPLICATION
- Encourage the children to solve open-ended problems devised by you or
  other children.
- Encourage the children to use process skills in a systematic way.
- Observe the children applying their ideas and using process skills and
  record significant examples.
- Provide opportunities for the children to discuss and to evaluate.

PROVIDING APPROPRIATE ACTIVITIES

The role of the teacher is a complex one and of paramount importance in helping children to develop their process skills and scientific concepts and encouraging and fostering positive attitudes to science. None of this happens by accident: the teacher has to provide the necessary opportunities for skills and understanding to develop.

The purpose of this stage is to start children thinking and organising their ideas. The starting point may be a story, a video, a television programme, a visit or a collection. This stimulus needs to be interesting with both familiar and unfamiliar materials to arouse interest and curiosity. Children work independently on their own or in small groups. The collection needs to be well organised and attractively displayed for children to examine on their own and explore for two or three days before the materials are used in elicitation activities.

Example:
In a topic on 'islands' the teacher has chosen to focus on materials and their properties. The initial stimulus, a collection of 'materials washed up on the beach', includes plastic, cork, wood, metal, rocks etc. The children are encouraged to handle the materials and have free access to the display.

This exploratory stage serves to help children find out and clarify what they think while enabling the teacher to assess their understanding in order to plan appropriate next steps. Work is with materials which (after orientation activities) are already familiar; children are encouraged to explore and refine their ideas. The emphasis is on 'handling' and 'doing', allowing children to engage in the exploration process skills. 'Brain-storming' of ideas with whole class, small groups or pairs is a good idea. Ideas can be written down in a 'mapping' form (see section on children's recording - Chapter 5). Sorting activities and initial exploration can be undertaken in small groups or pairs with time for discussion and feedback. Group's ideas can be recorded in a 'floor book'. It may take several weeks for the children to explore and initially try out each other's ideas.

Example:
The children handle items from the collection while they gather ideas during an initial whole class 'brain-storm'. What's in the collection? What materials are they made from? What are their properties? What are they used for? They compare different materials sorting them according to their own and the teacher's criteria. The children wonder how the objects got on the island. They explore 'floating/sinking' and the hardness of materials.

The children begin to develop and replace old ideas with new ones through investigation: they are encouraged to test and compare ideas in a more systematic way, using their investigative process skills. Children are generally more motivated when some ideas for testing come from them and not all from the teacher. Groups or pairs of children investigate ideas, testing more systematically. Time is given for them to discuss ideas in pairs, groups or as a whole class. Ideas, predictions and findings may be recorded in the 'floor-book' (Chapter 5). The children may need several weeks to develop or replace their existing ideas.

Example:
The children begin systematic testing of 'floating/sinking' with the idea that 'heavy things sink, light things float'. They challenge other ideas, testing the effect of water on materials (clay, wood, metal, rotting, rusting). They test hardness and porosity of materials and try purifying water etc.

Children should be encouraged to review what they have found out, discuss its significance and draw conclusions. They may review during an activity, at the end or after a series of activities. Small groups or pairs feed back to each other or to the whole class. Particular emphasis is put on the significance of what they have found out and on any changes in their thinking.

Example:
They review their findings and draw conclusions: a) Not all light things float, b) Air and shape have something to do with it, c) Rocks and sand do not rot in water but wood does.

Children are given open-ended problems to solve in order to see if they can apply and transfer acquired knowledge and skills. They are also encouraged to find their own problems to tackle. Small groups (three-four children) or pairs work together with less constant support from their teacher.

Example:
They are given a 'real' problem: The school sandpit needs cleaning. The teacher gives them a mixture of sand, powdered clay, gravel, wood and cork chippings. Some children solve the problem by adding water and sieving.

make decisions independently about what they are going to do next. The teacher has to move fluently with various changing currents while keeping a firm grip on the chosen Big Idea (the area of science towards which the teacher is working. Chapter 2, p.28), the aims of the scheme of work and physical constraints within the school. The uninitiated might see the teacher's role in such seemingly unpredictable circumstances as one of improviser, carried this way and that, unable to control events.

In fact the converse is true. Improvisation is what takes place when organisation fails, when the unexpected occurs. In the constructivist classroom it is not only expected, but required, that children make decisions for themselves. The teacher's responses are, in point of fact, as much planning-related as they would have been had the teacher made the decisions. Devolution in the chain of planning from a school's overall policy document down to the teacher's day journal ensures that all science activities in the classroom in a given period fall within an agreed area of the scheme of work, or are continuing under licence from a previous planned activity. This foreknowledge allows the teacher to predict, and to meet, likely demands on resources. At least, the limits of the resources will be known. The 'Big Idea' will have been chosen from the scheme of work in the light of medium-term planning decisions and the continuous assessment, embodied in Elicitation and Restructuring, will determine what individual children's learning needs are.

Therefore, when a child makes a decision, for example to investigate the strength of different fibres, against this planning background, the teacher's response becomes a matter of assessing all the known factors – relevance, desirability (within wide tolerances), and possibility – against the child's known learning needs and the implications for other children in the classroom. Every one of these factors is planning-related. So the teacher makes planning decisions continuously during pupil-contact time, and regularly at other times.

Another function of planning is to try to make sure that what children actually learn matches what is thought best for them to learn. This matching is commonly called 'Progression'. We say 'actually' learn because learning is not synonymous with passage through a field of knowledge or experience, as some people appear to think. As the relevant chapters will show, the continuous assessment and recording which is a characteristic of the constructivist approach, makes the monitoring of progression easy. It is a natural link between planning and practice and becomes the vehicle for the valuable 'loop-forward' of information into planning which completes the circle.

CHAPTER 2

Orientation

1. Introduction

Orientation has two main facets:

a) the stimulation of interest and curiosity
b) the beginning of the process of recognising ideas about the material presented. This process is continued and developed with teacher-intervention during elicitation/structuring (see Chapter 3). At the outset, however, the ideas emerge naturally from the children's direct experience.

In practice these two facets are interdependent, reciprocal and, obviously, stimulus-related. The teacher's job begins with the identification of starting points which will provide this stimulus. This chapter will deal with the nature of such starting points and will go on to consider the attitude of the teacher, the selection of activities within areas of science and the implications for classroom management and organisation.

2. The nature of starting points

Starting points can be thought of as the opening of gates to pathways along which repeated contact with the materials or events will be possible. Starting points include watching an event, handling a collection of objects, visiting a location, meeting a visitor, watching a video, listening to a story, engaging in drama or role-play, reading or exploring an environment or location. Note that the starting points are not the same as the destinations, or the journey along the pathway. Listening to a visitor speak, or visiting a location do not of themselves alone educate in any meaningful way. However, if the glimpses of what lies beyond the open gates are attractive enough, children will be highly motivated to follow the pathways that are revealed.

All starting points are gateways to the same set of pathways, as they might be in a National Park, if that is an adequate analogy of a Big Idea (an area of science). Provided the children's senses are alert, they will gradually become acquainted with what the park contains (the component ideas) no matter what sequence of paths they follow.

At the outset it is important that children enjoy their own responses to the starting points. The excitement of choosing a pathway and venturing along it is an essential part of developing and sustaining curiosity. Although the teacher's selection of a particular starting point will be a part of an overall plan, with a specific goal, there is no reason why that should restrict the children's first thoughts and first reactions. The part the teacher plays at this stage is minimal but important and is designed to do no more than prompt and encourage the children to start on their exploration, by one path or another. It should not be inferred from this that the teacher will keep his or her overall intentions a secret from the children. These will be included in any introduction the teacher may make in presenting the starting point. Once introduced however, it is the interaction of the children's senses and mind that is important while they decide what to focus on, what is significant. They will be observing, thinking, using secondary sources and discussing.

3. Classroom relationships start with the teacher

The relationship a teacher has with the children can help to make an activity a valuable learning experience; it can, equally, render it worthless. Whilst this, to some extent, is an individual affair for any teacher it is important that we each recognise ourselves through our teaching. The hidden and not so hidden fears that teachers might have can affect the quality of classroom interactions. Individual teachers' perceptions of how they are doing is necessarily, as Pollard explains (1985), a very subjective judgement:

18

> Of course people's perceptions of any situation will be patterned by various aspects of the culture around them, but for any individual there will be unique features depending on his or her biography, socialisation and previous experience. (Pollard, 1985)

In the classroom with thirty five children teachers seem to reveal themselves totally. The children see the worst and the best and their grasp of responses is intuitive. Children may not articulate their feelings well but their behaviour and reactions can be very illuminating.

The problem is that in their desire to please the teacher or to 'get things right' children will use their intuitive grasp as guidance. This can be detrimental to the constructivist approach. We have found that, even with experienced teachers, self-awareness does not necessarily match reality. Most teachers have personal teaching habits they are not aware of and are shocked if they find that others perceive them clearly. Sometimes, for example, there can be a tendency to use too many probing questions too early, possibly in an anxiety to get things moving quickly. What happens is that the child is given the impression that there is a right answer to be achieved. Sometimes the teacher bombards the child with too many questions and gives the impression that the child is expected to guess what the teacher is thinking. After all, children will be looking for a pattern in the questioning. Sometimes a request to children to repeat what they said can be interpreted as a request for a different statement as if what they said was wrong. The teacher may have had none of these intentions yet a message – a virtual direction – will have been passed to the children.

Reflective teachers, in collaboration with colleagues, can come to terms with their own 'biography', recognising the values they have acquired and their influence on the way they establish relationships in the classroom. The dividend paid for undertaking this personal exploration is manifest in the resulting secure infra-structure that holds relationships in the classroom together. The practical situations necessary for teaching science are most effective when they afford freedom for the children to explore their own ideas. Reflective teachers are best able to provide such an environment. (Examples of this are discussed in Chapter 8).

We are seeking to move from the idea of the teacher as an instructor who knows all the answers to the idea of a teacher as someone who challenges children to think, listens to their explanations of events and values them as revelations. However, it is vital to keep in mind that this does not mean that freedom to explore is a 'free-for-all', or that any old thing a child utters is significant. In the first place children need a clear sense of direction, notwithstanding the fact that they are navigating themselves. This requires appropriate challenges from the teacher whenever randomness becomes apparent. In the second place it is essential to remember that discoveries must make sense to the children themselves. To this degree, there are indeed 'right' answers. Elements must be seen to fit a pattern or not to fit. Where they do not fit some other action may be called for. Even at the informal orientation stage the teacher must avoid giving the impression that there is no purpose to the activity. The teacher who takes careful note of what children are actually saying, or are attempting to say, who genuinely values what is said, who challenges and prompts children to think logically at appropriate moments and to express their thoughts fearlessly, will inspire children to think and communicate and through these processes become constructors of their own knowledge. G. Wells (1976) emphasises the point that the desire to communicate promotes in children the art of formulating thoughts and feelings which itself becomes the strongest spur to trying actively to understand them.

All children are sustained by practical reinforcement of the value of their own ideas and reactions. Such reinforcement should be part of the teacher's working attitudes at all times and for all children. Simply to praise a child, 'That is very good – you've done well', 'That's an excellent piece of writing', 'Yes, you've got an original idea', is in itself not enough to convince children that you trust their thinking. That trust is demonstrated during the interaction that goes along with activities.

Our first case-study is based on an orientation activity that gradually becomes elicitation. It serves to illustrate the teacher's role and responses to the children as the activity develops. In this example the teacher, Ann Deakin of Milton Infants' School, Weston-Super-Mare, was working with a group of four-year-olds, Ben, Christopher, Jennifer, John, Katy and Nicola. Her contributions were in response to what the children said and her questions acted as encouragement for them to pursue their own ideas. The notes of the children's utterances were the teacher's own. It was a long case-study so sections have been paraphrased.

CASE-STUDY: EXPLORING FRUIT AND VEGETABLES

The children were handling a collection of vegetables for the first time. The children and teacher were sitting round a table. The table was protected by newspaper. The vegetables included: parsnips, carrots, mushrooms, tomatoes, cabbage, cucumber, leeks, beetroot, swede, onions and sprouts.

The teacher asked: 'Have you seen any of these before?' This introductory question gave rise to free exploration. The children were left to follow their own interests.

First responses included:

My guinea pig has this. (Carrot) This makes me cry. (Onion) I wonder what this smells like. (Leek) My rabbit likes this. (Carrot) This is like a scarecrow. (Carrot is held to the end of nose) This is like a small lettuce. (Sprout) This is a big nose. (Cucumber held to nose – another child says 'That's too big') What's this? (Swede. None of the children offered a suggestion – the question was directed at me so I replied) Look at my circle nose. (Onion) This is hard. (Cucumber) This is squidgy. (Mushroom) This is stinky winky. (Leek) We could eat these. (Cucumber, Tomato)

The children explored the properties and characteristics of the vegetables, comparing them with previous experiences.

The teacher joined in as John was looking at the leek to remind Ben that he might have seen one before. Ben had worn a leek on St. David's Day. They discussed the leek. The children commented that it was long and round. They then looked for and found other examples of long and round vegetables. Then a child described the mushroom as 'round with a white spout'. The teacher picked up on this to get the children to have a second and closer look at all the vegetables.

Teacher:	Is there anything else white?
Christopher:	This has. (Leek)
Teacher:	Let's put everything that has white into a set ring. The mushroom and leek go in.
Christopher:	This has white bits. (Carrot)
Christopher:	This is white. (Parsnip)
Christopher:	This is white. (Onion with a pale top)
John:	Has this white? (Cabbage) Yes the end is white.
Christopher:	This is white. (One half of Swede)

Jennifer: Nearly everything has white!

The teacher suggested that they put all vegetables with white together in a set and the remainder on one side. The children grouped them in the following way:

White - onion parsnip   Remainder - cucumber
     cabbage carrot   beetroot
     swede leek   tomato
     mushroom   sprout

The collection of vegetables in the set with 'white in' brought together some unexpected examples. This closer look had revealed more detail than first impressions.
   The teacher encouraged a further look at each of the vegetables. She asked them if they could think of another colour for sorting the vegetables. The teacher has begun to elicit specific ideas. Jennifer latched onto the way the previous sort had arisen and held up the cucumber:

Jennifer: Everything that's green.

The children found that the onion had a green shoot, the tomato a green top (sepals), the parsnip a green growth at the top and the leek had both light and dark green parts.

Green - cucumber tomato   Remainder - carrot
     onion parsnip   mushroom
     swede leek   beetroot
     cabbage sprouts

Then they tried to give them all a name. Ben was unsure about the parsnips so they all had a look.

Jennifer: It looks like a shaker (Maracas)

So far the children have been handling, looking and talking; they have compared the vegetables with other objects within their experience; they have noticed a similar characteristic that was not what they expected, and then they tried to name the vegetables. The teacher moved them on to using another of their senses. She began to say 'Now we can name them by looking.

Let's ...', and Jennifer interrupted 'Do it without looking'. They closed their eyes and felt the vegetables. The teacher asked 'How can you tell without looking?'

Jennifer: I can feel the shape.
John: I was going round and round with my hands.
Nicola: I sniffed it.

The teacher suggested a blindfold and asked Ben if he'd like to try.

Ben: A carrot. (It was a parsnip)

The teacher gave him a carrot to hold in the other hand.

Ben: A carrot.
Teacher: Do they feel the same?
Ben: Long. Long and fat at one end.
Teacher: Let's put the long ones in a set.

So they started to make another classification. The children have returned to an idea that they had explored earlier but this time the teacher encouraged them to create a set for each shape.

Christopher: This is round.
Teacher: We could have two sets.

The teacher put out two set circles and the children quickly sorted long and round.

Jennifer: This is round and has a long spout. (Mushroom). Where shall we put it?

After the children had decided that it could go in either set the teacher suggested that they overlap the rings so that it was in both.

parsnip	leek	mushroom	sprout	swede
cucumber			tomato	beetroot
carrot			cabbage	

Overlapping sets were introduced to the children for the first time.

In this activity a careful balance is achieved between the children's interest and the teacher's lead toward processes of observation, sorting and classifying. The children's early free-ranging comments were the result of a few minutes handling, while the teacher watched and listened. The children were not inhibited by any hidden pressure to do and say the right thing. This is due in part to the age of the children (not yet affected by the school system) as well as to the openness of the teacher to sharing experiences with the children. When she did join the conversation it was to remind Ben of another time he had handled a leek. In doing this she conveyed her interest in what happened to the children, and encouraged, by example, a way of thinking in which new and previous experiences could be linked.

The teacher's question: 'Is there anything else white?' arose from the interesting observation of one of the children that a mushroom has a white spout. Other experience of spouts, perhaps a tea-pot or a jug, had helped association of ideas in the observation. Again the teacher, by picking up on this child's contribution, has encouraged a linking of ideas. The hunt for white in the other vegetables required a really close look and took the children beyond their first thoughts. At the same time the children were being led towards the notion of 'sets' as a result of sorting. The search for similarities and differences is an important part of scientific and mathematical thinking. When the teacher then encouraged the children to create a new set, the colour green was chosen by Jennifer as she followed the teacher's example. The new hunt for evidence of green forced the children into another close encounter with the vegetables and a new set was created.

The next development in this activity, from looking to feeling, was taken enthusiastically out of the teacher's hands by Jennifer. Feeling the vegetables led to the creation of two sets and, with the help of the mushroom, to the idea of overlapping sets. The group of children moved smoothly from one sense focus to another and at the same time learned ways of organising their ideas. Throughout, the teacher conveyed her interest in the children's systematic observation and helped them to develop an approach to classification. Her talk with the children exemplified the four principles suggested by Gordon Wells (1986, p.50) as a useful guide to encouraging children's language development, by building on their willingness to communicate:

- When the child appears to be trying to communicate, assume he or she has something important to say and treat the attempt accordingly.
- Because the child's utterances are often unclear or ambiguous, be sure you have understood the intended meaning before responding.
- When you reply, take the child's meaning as the basis of what you say next – confirming the intention and extending the topic or inviting the child to do so him- or herself.
- Select and phrase your contributions so that they are at or just beyond the child's ability to comprehend.

The claims being made for this simple case-study might seem a bit exaggerated. The activity itself could appear to be one of many taking place every day in any infant class. It may indeed be so, but it may also be subtly different. This very early stage in the children's experience of school will lay the foundation for the future. The activity was commonplace; the persistence of the teacher in maintaining her interest in the children's ideas was not. Even a small change in the handling of this activity, for example if the teacher had asked the children to name the vegetables or had instructed them to sort them into different colours, then into shapes, would have set the teacher's agenda at the expense of the children's. The children would have completed the task in line with the teacher's thinking instead of undertaking their own enquiry. This would have made further activity and thinking on their part limited by dependence on the teacher and have implied a 'rightness' and 'wrongness' in their solutions.

The case-study now continues with the teacher following the children's lead, pursuing and encouraging the observation of texture and smell. Sensitive intervention by the teacher helps the children to extend their thinking, and her willingness to abandon her intention to develop smell in favour of looking, allow the children to work from their greater interest. That has the effect of increasing experience of the structure of vegetables:

Jennifer: We could make a person.

All the children helped and chatted about what they could use and between them produced a person with a pipe. The informal chat gave the opportunity for further handling and thinking.

2 mushroom eyes
1 tomato nose
1 cucumber mouth with carrot pipe
2 beetroot ears
3 sprout buttons
2 leek arms
2 carrot legs

One of the teacher's feely bags was a doll. The feely bag doll felt different from the vegetable doll. This provided an introduction to a feely bag game with the vegetables. Different vegetables were placed secretly into the second bag and children put their hands in to feel the contents.

Nicola:	I can feel it's soft, squish squashy, feel the circle. I can feel hairy things (Mushroom)
Christopher:	Long round squashy (Leek)
John:	I can smell the leek.

They all had turns at smelling. The teacher blindfolded herself and tried to guess which they were holding. (Mushroom, leek and onion). Some touched her face so she could tell by feeling. She was going to suggest that they cut up the vegetables in order to smell them better when a carrot broke. John announced that it had broken. With a slight change in her intended direction, she suggested that they should all have a close look at it.

Christopher:	The middle is darker.
Teacher:	Let's use a knife to cut some off.

Each child cut some off.

Jennifer:	It has a carrot skin – let's take off the skin.

John put the cucumber in his mouth and bit it. 'This has a skin'.
They agreed to cut up the cucumber.

Jennifer:	It's wet inside. You can smell the inside. It's lighter (in colour). Why not take the skin off the others and see what is inside?

This they did.

John:	(With a leek). It's white inside. It's getting white. It's gone like crystal.
Nicola:	(With a parsnip). It's white inside.
Katy:	I can't even cut it with a knife. (Swede) I can pull this off (Sprout).
	I've done it, it's greeny inside (Onion)
Christopher:	Look what I've done! (Leek completely in pieces)
Jennifer:	Look it's red.
Teacher:	Have you cut yourself?
Jennifer:	No, it's the juice from the beetroot

Ben took one skin off the onion

| Teacher: | What about the tomato? |

Christopher took off the skin, or tried to and all the middle came out onto the piece of paper. 'Oooh! It's gooey'.

The vegetables were left on a display table together with a magnifying glass for the children to have the opportunity for making individual observations at other times.

The activity had very successfully led the children from their first haphazard observations to an ordered development of their ideas. The basis of all that followed was in those early remarks: the sensations of seeing, smelling and touching. The manner in which the activity developed will be repeated many times by the teacher but each time the pattern of experiences and observations will enable children to undertake their own independent explorations. The latter part of this activity gave the children a further opportunity to clarify their ideas. Their additional comments continued the structuring of their ideas and gave the teacher further insight into their current understanding. This exploration will lead, eventually, to the process of systematic investigation.

The whole ethos of the classroom in which the teacher was free to work with a group of children, free from the demands of controlling resources and the behaviour of the other children, in which materials were accessible, derived from the teacher's enabling attitude to the children. The relationship that this teacher built up with the children was based on reciprocal trust and respect. The foregoing account of a constructivist-based approach could apply equally effectively to work in any area carried out in the tradition of an experienced-based curriculum. Its inclusion at this point is to reinforce the significance of its effect on the success of practical activities essential to science.

Summary

The responsive attitude of the teacher to both science and the children's learning is, in this example, fundamental to her relationship with the children. The relationship is the key to producing active, rather than passive, learners. Children who work only to the teacher's framework for understanding are more likely to remain passive learners and be dependent upon their ability to think like the teacher. It is at the early stage of handling new materials, whatever the age of the children, that this is most crucial. This time of 'orientation' requires free handling and free thinking.

While each child is getting to grips with ideas past, present and predicted, as a result of observation of the materials in hand, the teacher is undertaking a similar operation with the child as a focus. The teacher is also actively constructing ideas about the children, their attitudes, approaches, skills and existing ideas. A teacher can become expert at picking up disjointed signals and flashes of inspiration from the exploring children as they attempt to match ideas with the language at their command and, in so doing, find ways to help the children to establish explanatory links between their developing thoughts. The 'child in focus' is a recurring theme throughout the book and central to constructivist strategies.

4. The selection of orientation activities within an area of science

Selecting orientation activities starts by identifying the 'Big Ideas' related to the area of science to be studied. These Big (scientific) Ideas determine the smaller, component ideas which can then become the focus of activity in the classroom. The starting points – the opening gates – will relate to the component ideas. The pathways subsequently taken by the children will meander through the National Curriculum programmes of study related to the chosen Big Ideas.

Example: Attainment Target 3. Materials and their properties

Big Ideas related to Materials could be divided into three parts and identified as follows:

Properties and uses:	Materials have different properties that make them more or less suitable for different purposes.
Changes:	Materials can be changed to make them either more or less suited to particular purposes (i.e. wood can be varnished or it can rot). Some changes can be reversed, others are irreversible, but material cannot be created from nothing; or reduced to nothing; it can only be changed from one form to another.
States of matter:	Materials can exist in solid, liquid or gaseous forms (e.g. ice, water, water vapour) and when they change from one form to another, energy is either required or released.
	(Parker-Rees, Thyer, Ollerenshaw, 1991)

Clearly these 'Big Ideas' are not intended to represent an expectation of understanding by children in the primary school. What they do represent is the purpose behind a teacher's planning so that the value of children's different pathways may be identified and used.

The above 'Big Ideas' for materials could be used to determine the following orientation opportunities:

Materials – Properties and uses

A suitable collection of objects should include a range of materials – rocks, slate, tile, brick, roof felt, insulation material, fabric, timber, wooden artifacts, paper, synthetic material (plastic, polystyrene), containers (paper, card, wood, metal). Such a collection includes some objects that are familiar and linked with a child's experience, and some that are unfamiliar but have intrinsic appeal. Some objects trigger 'component ideas' about the similarities and differences between processed and natural materials, between materials that have been treated and protected, such as wood which has been varnished, or untreated wood that can rot. Ideas about the suitability of a material for its use can be compared.

Introducing the collection to children is an important stage in the orientation process. The collection needs to be attractively displayed to invite handling. Children could work independently, either on their own or in small groups, exploring the materials. The materials could be available for use in this way for two or three days before being used in elicitation activities.

One teacher whose topic was 'Building' had accumulated a huge range of building materials (some of the school was being rebuilt and housing estates around the school were under construction). These materials were arranged on all the main display surfaces in the classroom for almost two weeks before they were used for elicitation and development work. During this time the year four (nine-year-old) children had opportunities to handle and discuss the materials, recognise those that they had seen around in construction work, at home or in school and so on. By the time their ideas were elicited in a more structured way by the teacher the children's impressions, questions, comparisons and predictions had already taken shape.

Other collections that could be used for 'properties and uses' might be: wooden objects, cleaning materials, metals, natural products, synthetic products. The ultimate choice of a collection may be influenced by the availability of materials and the intended topic work, if there is a topic.

The way children are invited to handle a collection is important. Even though the teacher wants the children to begin thinking and organising their own ideas this is best undertaken with a clear sense of purpose. The purpose can be explained by the teacher. For example: 'This collection involves many objects made from many different materials. We are hoping to learn something about these materials in the next few weeks – how they are made and what they can do and why. You may have seen some of them before. Many of them are to be used in the school building programme. Handle them, look closely and find out what you notice about them'.

Further aspects of the Big Ideas related to materials could suggest the following starting points:

Materials – Changes

A suitable collection of objects should include natural materials and materials that have undergone different processes of change – timber, varnished wood, sheep's wool, knitting wool, sand, cement, concrete, cotton thread/fabric, charcoal, bread, toast. The use of this collection could lead to exploring what happens to the materials if they get *wet, hot, frozen, stretched* or *bent*, and identifying which materials have been processed, how they have been changed and why.

Materials – Changes/States of matter

Physical events provide opportunities to watch things change. Unlike handling a collection there is little physical interaction with the objects but just as much observation and thinking. It is probable that the same event will be experienced more than once – the first time for orientation, when the ideas come freely, and the next time with guided and supported elicitation. For example:

- The process of melting – ice cubes, wax, chocolate, margarine and cheese, may all be contained in plastic bags and immersed in hot and then cold water. This would provide the opportunity to see what happens as the materials change and whether melted materials will become solid again.
- The process of dissolving – sugars, salts, jelly, flour, powder paint, talc and baking powder, could be added to water or have water added to them. The changes could be monitored to see whether the material disappears, whether the water changes, and if it does, how?
- Heating and cooling – egg, ice, steam, wax, chocolate, margarine, cheese can be heated or cooled. Changes between solid, liquid and gas could be identified including the direction of possible change.

In introducing an event teachers should offer a purpose for watching: For example, 'We are going to learn something about the materials that are all around us. There are differences and similarities about them that we will try to find a way to explain. Spend some time watching what happens; think about what is happening and talk to your friends about it'. Once again the children will then be left to proceed as they see fit. Even if teachers are around (for safety reasons) they should resist too much involvement with conversations at this stage.

Appropriate starting points for the other Attainment Targets could be generated in a similar way. First read the programme of study, identify the Big Ideas that lie behind the activities suggested in the programme of study (this may require some research), and then plan starting points and materials that will provide pathways among the component ideas. The suggestions above are included only as an example of this way of planning; they are not intended as tips for activities. There are many more possible starting points and they are best linked with children's experiences in and out of the classroom.

Children talking

Whatever the materials or situation it is the children's ideas that are sought. Whether the prompt from the teacher is formal or informal the children's curiosity is at stake. The case-studies that follow include:

(1) *A collection of toys and kitchen tools* to explore ideas about force in simple mechanisms; that things can be moved by pushing and pulling them:

Big Ideas: Movement. When a force is applied to an object the movement energy of the object is changed. A force can make things move faster, more slowly or change direction. Machines can help us to apply forces in ways which would not otherwise be possible.

(2) *A collection of shiny things* to explore ideas about the way that light reflects from objects:

Big Ideas: Forms of energy. Light moves between a source and its visible effect. Light bounces off objects.

(3) *Pond water* – an event to include children watching for signs of life as an introduction to work on habitat and feeding:

Big Ideas: Similarities and differences between living organisms reflect the different environments to which they are adapted and the different solutions that have proved successful in meeting basic needs.

We next give some case-studies of orientation sessions in action.

CASE STUDY 1: EXPLORING TOYS

A group of five-year-olds was presented with *a collection of toys* that included a range of working mechanisms. The children were free to handle them and try them out. They were encouraged to look carefully at the toys to find out how they worked. This part of the activity lasted about twenty minutes. The children's comments revealed an awareness of the relationship between movement and a force. Typical comments included:

Sarah:	You've got to pull that thing.
Chris:	(By) pushing that.
Chris:	You've got to wind it up.
Robert:	The air goes into the hole – you squeeze it.
Sarah:	You've got to turn that and it makes a funny noise.
Heather:	You press those end bits and it moves.
Heather:	You pull the bell and its feet go up.
Chris:	You pull that little thing out and it moves.

This orientation opportunity actually elicited the early structuring of the children's ideas. The wide-ranging responses included the points that will be the teacher's focus for more structured elicitation. The children noticed the link between something happening and the push, pull, press or squeeze (force) that was required. This handling time gave them the chance to become familiar with the objects, to use their prior experience to inform their first impressions and to begin to find language to describe what they noticed. The second part of the orientation activity was started by the teacher who picked up one toy and asked the children to find other toys that worked in a similar way. The children systematically worked through the collection, sorting and grouping in this way until they had created sets, subsequently labelled, that required a similar force to work: 'Pull', 'Push', 'Turning', 'Pressing', 'Jumping' and 'Wiggly'. During the very active sorting the children tried matching the movement of one toy with another. Because this collection was high in 'play appeal' the teacher felt some focusing of thought appropriate about half way through when she started the sorting process off. This may seem more like an elicitation activity (see Chapter 3) but the intention here was not for the teacher to select a focus but to help the children to make links between their observations. Even so, what followed came from the children.

The whole activity lasted around forty minutes. The group were visited by the teacher when she introduced the collection, again, twenty minutes later when she listened in for a few minutes and intervened (as above) and then again after a further fifteen minutes. At the third visit the children explained their grouping of the toys. At that point the children were poised to begin the next phase of activity when the teacher would attempt to elicit greater detail in their observations as they began to explain why things happened and voice ideas in a more specific way. It is likely that a selected part of the original collection would help to focus developing ideas in the ensuing elicitation phase.

Regrettably often, classroom activities cease after exploration such as this. All we have found out is the beginning of what the children already know and can do. The children have revealed an understanding of what helps things to move and, at the same time, demonstrated already established process skills such as observing, communicating, comparing and sorting. For the children's understanding to be extended the teacher must move the children on from these demonstrated ideas and skills and present a new challenge. For there to be progression in learning the children must be supported, through elicitation, in discovering more precisely, what they already understand and think. They will then need help in 'restructuring' their ideas. (Chapter 4).

CASE-STUDY 2: EXPLORING KITCHEN TOOLS

A class of ten-year-olds were due to begin a half-term topic on 'Other People'. They were to consider other people's homes and, in particular, kitchens. The science theme was to be linked with aspects of energy and forces, exploring the Big Ideas mentioned earlier. As a result three groups of children were presented with *collections of kitchen tools* – many with moving parts. As in the previous example the teacher made a brief introduction of the materials to the children and revisited them later in the session.

The children spent about half an hour handling the tools and discussing their uses. Many of the tools were novel and unfamiliar to the children. The children attempted to explain how they worked and then began to group tools that worked in a similar way. They did this without prompting, having worked in this way previously. Once again the children tried to communicate their ideas in their own words. These particular children were considered as likely to experience difficulties in communicating.

The children once again identified force in action and referred to; 'push', 'pull', 'spin', 'squeeze', 'push and pull', 'squeeze and spin'.

Darren: You twist the handle (cheese grater)

Nicola: Squeeze it down (icing piper)

Lenny: You get hold of the handle and pull it along (pastry cutter)

Nicola: Push it in and it picks it up (tongs)

Lenny: No. Slowly close the handles, then you twist (tin opener)

Emma: Push it. You put it on top and then you push it. ... They circles go in they gaps and makes it move.

Nicola: You've got to spin that. It goes onto these little ones and it goes down into those (blades) (egg whisk)

Darren: You squeeze that (tongs)

Darren: You push it so icecream goes in and then push button and the icecream comes out (icecream scoop)

Lenny: You get your fingers in and move 'em up and down (scissors)

The children had given close attention to the mechanisms. The way they expressed themselves focused on the important idea of force and movement. The language used could now be put in a more limited context and used to help the children examine force in action and its effects. The handling activity was followed by further exploration: the children tried out three tools for whisking and thought about which one made work easiest and why. This brought forth explanations of why and how some movements made work easier. These, in turn, focused their earlier comments as they tried to bring their free-ranging ideas together. It is interesting to note that the comments of the older children are not dissimilar from those of the younger children (in CS1) at this orientation stage of the work. The difference between them is likely to emerge as the children work their way towards investigations in which they control variables and take measurements.

CASE-STUDY 3: EXPLORING SHINY THINGS

A group of six-year-old children worked with a *collection of shiny things*. They were invited to have a look at the objects and to begin to sort them out. The range of materials was large and included some mirrors. The teacher withdrew and the children began examining the items and talking about them.

The observer's notes showed that early in the handling of the objects a child commented that 'shiny things reflect'. This 'reflect' was linked with the reflection of an image. The children noticed that images were distorted in some surfaces, and that in others they were split. It was observed that when something was 'all scratchy' the reflection could not be seen so well: 'You can see the colour but not my face'. They found a number of shiny objects that did not allow them to see their reflections and others that did. The children did not distinguish between these objects and ended up where they had started, 'shiny things reflect' (an image) – in spite of evidence to the contrary.

During the elicitation/structuring activity that followed the teacher pressed the children to make closer comparisons and draw further, more accurate conclusions as a result. She reduced the number of objects and pursued a more specific enquiry as in the other case-studies.

CASE-STUDY 4: EXPLORING POND WATER

A class of eight-year-olds about to begin work in the area of Living Processes was presented with some tanks of water. The teacher, Amanda Tuck of Upper Horfield Primary School, Bristol, who had accustomed the class to exploratory approaches, simply said to them, 'What's this, then, Science Detectives?' The teacher's question was addressed to all or any of the children. The children had already organised their own working programmes so many of them were busy. Some, free at the time, picked up on the activity straight away; others came to it later in the week.

The children's observations took in many aspects of the inhabitants of the water. Their comments ranged wide and went well beyond the perfunctory labelling of recognised items.

Teacher:	What's this, then, Science Detectives?
Ben:	Well, it's not just water. It has snails in too, and pond weed.
	What's that dark thing in there? (to Michael).
	You can't really see it (puts it in the plastic magnifying box).
	We know what that is; it's a leaf.
David:	It's water-logged.
Ben:	Frizzled (looks through the microscope).
	It looks like prickles (about pond weed).
	Put it in here.
Mark:	What is that?
Ben:	I don't know. We're finding out. That's why we're here.
Paul:	It's a pond snail.
Ben:	A water snail. I'm going to look at him (looks at him through magnifier).
Paul:	You're blocking the light.
Hannah:	What's this stuff? Snails or something? (Joins the group and observes).
Ben:	(Looking at weed) In the microscope his looks like holly (laughter – there was a 'Holly' in the class).
Hannah:	Water snails are horrible.
Ben:	No, they're not; they're interesting.
Hannah:	It's moving (looks). It's little.
Ben:	One's stuck to the glass.

Sarah:	They've got suckers.
Ben:	Have they? (Looking) It's moving. It looks like a worm to me.
David:	Let's see it moving. O.K. (looks).
Ben:	It's walking. Moved again. It's going down the slider ...
David:	If you look underneath (the snail) you can see a hole. (Looks at another). There's a hole under all of them.
Ben:	It's slimy.
	There's lines on top of it (looking at the snail). There's yellow on it.
Rachel:	These have got spots on.
	They've got some yellow on the side.
Jo:	The water is green.
Rachel:	Some of them are thin and some are fat.
Ben:	They've got lines on too. They're brown.
Rachel:	They're all different colours.

Gradually the children's observations focused in more detail on the tank's occupants. Prior knowledge informed their watching, surprising details broadened their perceptions. The questions raised arose from the children's interest. The freedom with which the children talked and their preparedness to add their own ideas to a general discussion allowed them all to become more familiar with the animals in the water. This freedom was valued and fostered by the teacher. Each child had a contribution to make – and did so. Subsequent investigations picked up some of these early observations for enquiry. These included picking up on the topics of the colour of the snails and the way that helps to camouflage them, their preferred habitat and where snails were to be found, the structure of their bodies, the 'holes' underneath and the way their bodies were adapted for their environment.

5. Classroom management and organisation

Whether children are working individually or within small or large groups they require freedom to access equipment as it is needed. Independence of this kind requires that children are well practised in their use of equipment, returning it to its storage place when they have finished and clearing away after an activity.

Orientation activities can involve the whole class as a group: going on a visit, receiving a visitor, hearing a story or undertaking role play. They can involve the whole class working at the same time but in separate groups. Each group might work with a collection or an event and these could be similar or different. This arrangement is heavy on resources and difficult to manage if all the groups are moving around and trying things out.

Alternatively only a part of the class might be involved at any one time. This group could then be broken into two or three smaller groups of children, making things generally easier to manage in terms of equipment and resources. But it does raise the question 'What do I do with the rest of the children?' Working and moving around a class of children as they work in groups presents problems if the children are teacher-dependent for equipment and discussion. The teacher needs to be in a position to choose how to spend time to best advantage and should not be driven by resource and behaviour management alone.

A class may have six or seven groups of children working. If two of the groups are working with orientation activities two or three other groups may be finishing off previously started work in, say, language, requiring minimal teacher support other than occasional advice. The remaining two groups could engage in totally self-sustaining activities. These might involve book research for the area of the science topic. For activities of this kind the self-sustaining children need to be accustomed to using established strategies for finding spellings and meanings of words, for using index and content pages and so on. Overall this means that the orientation activities will create the most movement, the follow-up work a little movement and the language activity almost no movement. In this way movements should not prove disruptive and the demands on the teacher can be managed to best effect.

The teacher should spend a few minutes introducing orientation activities, move to the second activity, check that all is well, take an interest in the research activities and then return to orientation. The teacher may make a few notes of what is going on and intervene with a prompt question if it is really necessary. This may involve ten minutes. The teacher may then spend some time attending to needs that have arisen elsewhere in the room. Fifteen minutes or so later the teacher can return again to the orientation groups. Orientation time is not teacher-intensive but, as we have already mentioned, it does require an introduction to inspire the children to begin activity and give them a reason for proceeding.

Organisation of Resources

In order that children might learn to work in an independent way resources must be visible, accessible, clearly labelled and in a place of their own. There are resources that will be needed on a regular basis and these are best stored in the classroom. Other equipment that may have a specialised or less common use or is in short supply may be stored in a school's central resource. A set of collections could also be held in a central resource and used for a term or a half-term by individual classes. Even though collections will have regular use it will be by different classes or groups of children.

It is essential for each class to have its own supply of magnifiers as well as measuring equipment for capacity, mass, force, length and time. A well organised supply of everyday materials for general use during explorative and investigative work is invaluable.

Organising everyday materials

A home-made storage unit can be made from strong cardboard boxes (try the wine merchant). These can be piled and stacked two or three high and stuck together to make a block of six or nine. A flap on each box, folding up from the bottom, can be fixed into place. This will help to prevent materials falling out and will support a label. Two coats of emulsion paint or 'contact' covering will enhance the appearance of the storage. Everyday materials are best stored ready sorted. Labelling for young children could be pictorial and indicate the contents of different boxes, with drawings of a cube, cuboid, sphere, cylinder, string, wire and metal etc.

The prior sorting and labelling of materials not only prevents time wasting on fruitless searches through jumbled objects and obviates children being side-tracked by an interesting item – it also generates a more ordered approach to work by demonstrating the benefits of care and thought. The care which children take over the use of resources is dependent upon a responsible attitude being inculcated by the teacher's approach. If items are stored suitably and clearly labelled the message to the user is that organisation matters and is an important part of what they are doing. Training children to use items with care and return them to their storage place will become easier if the storage system supports them in the first place. Open, well labelled shelves, drawers and junk storage, are the starting points for the development of good classroom practice.

Summary

Orientation is an introductory phase associated with starting points for a given area of study. For the sake of clarity it has been dealt with separately from subsequent phases of the model. In reality, as is shown in the various case-studies, there is overlap in the classroom between orientation and elicitation activities. Hard and fast rules are not appropriate. It is common for insufficient time to be allowed for this important phase of work. Its value in establishing a foundation for a child's thinking is often underestimated.

Implicit in the way of working that we suggest is the belief that process skills used during exploratory and investigative activities are inextricably linked with acquisition of knowledge and that children best achieve understanding through their use. The orientation phase is no exception; the work that develops from these starting points is dependent upon both the area of knowledge identified by the teacher and the process skills that will service enquiry. Some activities provide greater opportunity for acquisition of knowledge, some for practising process skills, but both elements are interwoven.

CHAPTER 3
Elicitation

1. Introduction

Like children, when adults try to explain new experiences or understand new ideas we often find that we are not at all clear about what we already think. Our existing ideas are not always well organised and are often somewhat vague. As teachers, it is our job to support children in the crucial task of consciously discovering what it is they already think. This is a necessary first step for them to effect changes in their understanding. The supportive dimension of this role is particularly important when children discover their existing ideas are inadequate in that they do not explain situations, or when they find their ideas are inconsistent or contradictory. Children who remain confident, despite perhaps embarrassing revelations, will be able to take an active part in the reconstruction and modification which will be necessary for further learning. Particular teaching strategies will be needed if we are to support children in this way and share their unfolding ideas. As children actively construct their understanding of the experiences they have, we also must construct understanding; in our case it is understanding of the children's developing concepts, process skills, and the way they approach scientific activities, in order to make decisions about the next step in their learning.

Ausubel urges us to a similar view of children's learning. He encapsulates the approach which has subsequently been reinforced by many others including Harlen (1985, p.72; 1992, p.15), Driver (1983), Driver, Guesne and Tiberghien (1985), Osborne and Freyberg (1985), the National Curriculum Council (1989, A7):

⟩ The most important single factor influencing learning is what the
learner already knows; ascertain this and teach him accordingly.
(Ausubel 1968, p.685).

This chapter deals with the strategies needed for this elicitation
phase of a constructivist approach. We begin with a reminder
of why the elicitation phase is so important in learning,
particularly in science, and recognise that elicitation, certainly
in terms of children structuring their own ideas, is happening
throughout scientific exploration and investigations. We next
examine the part that observation plays in elicitation. Through
classroom examples we discuss a range of different strategies
for helping children organise and share their ideas. Issues related
to classroom organisation and management as well as to the ethos
of the classroom and the relationship between the teacher and the
children are also relevant to successful elicitation, as we illustrated
in Chapter 2 with reference to orientation. When we are trying to
find out what ideas children hold, their use of language becomes
very important. Can we take children's language at face value or
do we need to look beyond the actual words they are using? We
need to recognise the place of children's informal conversation
and the role of the teacher in facilitating and sometimes inhibiting
children's conversation. We will also look at the insights we can
gain into children's existing ideas from signals other than spoken
or written language. What can the way they behave and handle
materials tell us?

We then look at the origins of children's existing ideas. This
section considers the nature of children's experiences in and out
of school and explores the significance of what we call informal
and formal experiences in children's cognitive development.
There is little doubt, from the evidence in the case-studies, that
children's existing ideas, which certainly will not always match
accepted scientific ideas, are often firmly held and resistant to
change. We might therefore ask: do children deal with informal
and formal experiences in the same way? The nature of children's
existing ideas leads to the notion of children's common alternative
ideas, which are well-documented by teachers and researchers.
These are ideas that are often intuitive and naive in terms of
current scientific understanding but are found to be held by
children in different parts of the country, and, indeed, in different
countries. An awareness of these common ideas can be helpful to

teachers in anticipating and dealing with the particular needs of the children in their class.

There is a close relationship between elicitation and formative assessment since both are concerned with gaining an insight into children's learning in order to facilitate further learning.

2. What is elicitation and why is it important?

As we found in Chapter 2, when children first meet new materials or experiences in the classroom their first impressions and initial ideas are usually random and free-ranging. Without time to think through their own and, perhaps, other people's ideas, children are not ready to exploit the process of science to gain new or improved understanding. Elicitation is the time we provide for them to do just that: to build on the work they have done in the time given for orientation; to unravel and clarify their first impressions; to look for connections between these first impressions and previous experiences and ideas; to structure and organise what they think and compare it with the ideas of others. This is the opportunity to focus upon the science aspects of their wide-ranging ideas. Time is a key word since, quite often, despite what we may imagine goes on in our classrooms, children do not always get time to think. As one six-year-old was reported to have said when asked by a teacher what he thought about something, 'I only think when I go out to play!'. Another comment from a child, this time a nine-year-old, reminds us of the significance of language, particularly talk, as a means of organising ideas: 'How do I know what I think until I hear myself say it?'. Some children, and adults, say they talk to themselves when trying to solve a problem or understand phenomena.

Elicitation can be regarded as the time when children begin to focus their thinking. Schiller (1979) described experience as:

> ... immense like the ocean, it proliferates all round us. We cannot attend to the whole; at any one time we give attention at the most to a fraction. Something attracts attention, and observation sharpens its focus on one particular piece of experience; slowly we begin to perceive the significance of this piece, we grasp it, we apprehend it and assimilate it. We learn nothing from mere exposure to experience; learning comes when attention and

observation select, perception penetrates, and the significance of a particular piece of experience is grasped, it is apprehended and assimilated.

Children can be helped to focus and discern what is significant in their vast oceans of experience. In providing this assistance, however, we must recognise that we are serving two purposes. For the learners this clarification of what they already think is helping them become confident constructors of new ideas. It is making them more aware of their own thought processes and encouraging them to reflect upon and be critical of what they already think – are their existing ideas consistent, contradictory or incomplete? For us, as teachers, it provides insight into their existing ideas so that we can make appropriate interventions. These interventions may, as we saw in Chapter 2, be in terms of questions, facilitating discussion, or supporting the child in planning the next stage of their scientific work, or encouraging them to check out their ideas or challenging their existing ideas through new experiences or ideas. Although this might suggest that elicitation is a phase that occurs at a certain stage of children's scientific work, and this is a view of elicitation common in the literature about constructivism (Scott, 1987), it would be wrong to think that it happens once and for all in a particular activity. Learners continue to structure and clarify their ideas throughout their scientific work and in that sense we should continue to support this process, recognising also the continuing insights offered into the learners' thinking. It is perhaps useful, as suggested in Chapter 1, to consider the elicitation phase as that stage of the teaching process when the aim is both to help the learners structure their existing ideas, and at the same time, to enable the teacher to find out what the learner already thinks and can do.

3. What part does observation play during elicitation?

Observation is a skill which has a particular significance in science activities and, as Schiller recognised, is a fundamental aspect of focusing attention during experience. Often, observation is regarded as the starting point for science, and the scientific process is simplified as: observe, question, hypothesise, test and evaluate. This is, however, to fail to recognise the essential part observation plays throughout scientific exploration and investigation, and that sometimes hypotheses can arise from intuition rather than observation. The following tentative progression was outlined to help teachers in supporting children's observations throughout scientific activities (Ollerenshaw, 1992a):

(i)   First thoughts – naming, labelling, checking out;
(ii) Second thoughts – comparing like with like according to their use and properties, checking out;
(iii) Looking closer – differences between the similar items, checking out;
(iv) Seeing more – different ways to think and group, checking out;
(v)   Delving deeper – focusing on an object, watching, recording, comparing, explaining, checking out.

This was an attempt, whilst recognising that children's thinking will not always follow predictable pathways, to look at observation as a process which could, and perhaps should, be systematic and methodical. It also emphasises the importance of encouraging children to 'check out' at each stage and not to accept first impressions or perceptions. Equally important is the need to remember that observation involves more than just looking; it is a process in which children should be encouraged to use all their senses, in an attempt to build a comprehensive view of particular phenomena or materials, and structure ideas about them based on all the sensory information taken in.

The significance of observation to elicitation is, we hope, obvious; it is often through appropriate observation that children structure their ideas and share them with us, their teachers. Children's observations, like scientists', are inextricably tied to the existing ideas they hold. Observations are not, as some would have us believe, objective, but are more accurately described as 'theory-laden' (Wellington, 1989, p.7). What we look for, and what we see, are the result of what we already think and therefore expect to see. For example, children, and in the authors' experience, adults too, when working with simple circuits, commonly claim that a small electric lamp lights up when two connections are made to the bottom of the base, even when the evidence of their own activity contradicts this. In fact, the lamp only lights when one connection is made to the bottom and one to the side of the base. Intuitively, their personal theory is based on the idea that 'you connect bulbs at the bottom' and this is what they expect to observe and, in a sense, do 'observe'. Another example, noted by a Y6 teacher, concerned children's drawings of the inside of a flower. First attempts, before any discussion or teacher intervention on pollination and structure, were very different from drawings made later, in terms of what they focused upon and noticed.

4. Elicitation in action

The following case-study is an example of a teacher using children's observations as part of an elicitation phase of her teaching, during which she was encouraging the children to formulate their ideas about how sounds are produced (Attainment Target 4) and noting aspects of their existing ideas, related to the role of air in the working of wind instruments and the nature of vibrations, for future development. This case-study has similarities with the 'Fruit and Vegetable' orientation activity in Chapter 2. Both illustrate the bridge between orientation and elicitation but in this one we focus upon the strategies the teacher uses to extend elicitation in preparation for designing an investigation. Chapter 4 explains how investigation builds on the outcomes of elicitation.

CASE-STUDY: EXPLORING MUSICAL INSTRUMENTS

Three seven-year-old girls, Monique, Salama and Leah from Cabot Primary School in Bristol had been given a collection of instruments, from a variety of countries, to explore. The teacher, Pat Thomas, let them use the instruments in an unstructured way for about fifteen minutes, by way of orientation, occasionally listening in on the group to note down comments. Many of the children's utterances were labelling and descriptive but she considered some were significant in terms of the use of particular words, or predictions and implied hypotheses:

Monique: The thick strings make a bigger sound. (Zither)

Salama: No, it's a low sound and the thin strings make a high sound.

Leah:	It makes an echo. (Triangle).
Monique:	I think there are little seeds (inside) and when you shake it they bang against the side. (Shaker).
Salama:	A little nut moves when you blow. (Tin whistle).

At this stage the teacher joined the group for a more structured discussion. She asked the children to talk about the instruments, how they were played, what they were made from and where they came from. Her involvement encouraged the children to organise their ideas more explicitly. Comments at this point included:

Salama:	You have to blow your air in, if you cover up the hole at the top it doesn't play.
Monique:	The air makes a wind sound.
Salama:	Some air comes out of the holes and when you cover some of the holes up it sounds different. (Tin whistle).

Salama is focusing beyond her initial observations and beginning to offer explanations. The teacher left the group with an invitation to sort the instruments, suggesting they start by thinking about which were made from the similar materials. The group, who were used to working collaboratively, quickly achieved this and argument about the instruments which included more than one material was resolved by deciding to sort according to the material that 'there was most of'. By the time the teacher rejoined them they had re-sorted the instruments again according to how they were played. Further discussion elicited the language the children were using to describe this: blowing, scraping, plucking, shaking and banging. The teacher was given the opportunity to take the children further when Leah made a contribution having observed the metal prongs of the vibra:

Leah:	When you press it, it moves up and down; it wiggles.

At this point the teacher focused all of the children's observations and invited them to feel the strings of the other 'plucked' instruments and they used words such as, tickly, tingly and twangy. Leah moved the group forward again with:

Leah:	I think the drum moves.

The session finished with Leah being invited to test out her idea by observing the effect of rice on the drum's surface when it was hit. The teacher left the group with something to think about by striking a tuning fork and holding it on the surface of the water tank.

In this case-study we have evidence of selective and purposeful intervention from the teacher enabling the children to express their ideas, to explore the words they might use, to use the senses of sight, touch and hearing, and to sustain their curiosity. From the teacher's perspective, the time she spent with the group provided evidence of their existing knowledge and understanding, and hence a starting point for further investigative work. Two obvious opportunities arose which could be and were taken further. Salama's ideas about the wind instruments subsequently led to investigations with a range of wind instruments (including dismantling them) and an appreciation that the 'nut' was not always needed in an instrument that works by blowing. The initial ideas the children had about vibrations were the focus for a range of further experiences and investigations into the effect of string thickness and drum size, during which the children clarified their understanding of high/low, loud/quiet rather than big/small sounds.

5. How do we elicit children's ideas?

There are many ways of eliciting children's existing ideas and this section discusses some of them, with examples of teachers using them in their classrooms. The role of children's language, including their questions, is important and although aspects of this will be addressed through the case-studies it will be revisited later in the chapter.

a. Observing children during free or structured activities

We have already seen examples of teachers observing children during the introductory, unstructured, stage of an activities. The teacher working with the musical instruments began by listening to the group's chat as they explored the collection. This strategy requires a teacher to free herself to 'visit' a group or perhaps to observe from a distance to see how the children are handling or using materials and equipment. For example, young children working on the carpet with construction equipment and trying to make a vehicle can provide their teacher with an immediate insight into their understanding of axles and how wheels turn. Language is not always necessary. Another group, working with a collection of fabrics, provide insights for their teacher by the way they handle the collection, rubbing samples against their faces, pulling fibres from the edges and holding each piece up to a window. Actions such as these are pointers to the nature of the children's existing ideas.

Sometimes children's existing ideas can be elicited in unexpected contexts. A student teacher had asked a four-year-old to draw a picture illustrating a story she had just read about a drowning teddy bear who was saved by a sea gull which carried him home. Sally had drawn the bear in the gull's beak up in the sky. In the sea was another bear. 'What's this?', asked the teacher. 'That's teddy's reflection', replied the child. This provided a starting point for unanticipated elicitation and within a few minutes Sally had shared her ideas about reflection with her teacher and was exploring with a mirror. A spontaneous opportunity for science had been taken up by a vigilant teacher.

As contexts for eliciting children's ideas drama, movement and PE, for some children, can be less threatening than other means. Expressing ideas in role-play or through actions has been found by some teachers to allow a freedom of expression not possible through more formal classroom interactions. Work in a movement session focused on balance can reveal children's ideas about forces, for example: pushes, pulls, twists, equal and opposite forces, pivoting and balance (Howard, 1992).

b. Talking and listening to children

The most usual way of eliciting children's ideas is to listen to what they have to say or to engage in a dialogue with them. This can be on a one-to-one basis, informally during classroom activities, in a more systematic way through regular reviewing

(Ritchie, 1991a), or in small group or class discussions. All of these contexts are likely to be used by a sensitive teacher during a period of scientific work. Small group discussions have, perhaps, the greatest potential as a practical and effective strategy for eliciting ideas in a busy classroom setting.

The group working with the instruments were encouraged to engage in a more structured discussion when their teacher joined them and this provided her with new insights. Their comments were noted on a pad the teacher kept with her. However, the discussion need not be so structured and the teacher can join the children as an 'equal' partner during informal discussion. This can allow the children more control of the conversation's agenda, enabling them to make links that might well be inhibited by working solely to the teacher's agenda. Barnes (1976, p.29) attaches a lot of significance to this aspect of children's talk:

> The more a learner controls his own language strategies, and the more he is enabled to think aloud, the more he can take responsibility for formulating explanatory hypotheses and evaluating them.

The following case-study illustrates a conversation in which children were given control, although the teacher participated. The discussion went in a direction unanticipated by the teacher but was revealing, giving her insights into the children's ideas about materials (Attainment Target 3), which was her aim. Kathy Knowles, the teacher, is the science co-ordinator at Southville Primary School in Bristol.

CASE-STUDY: CHANGES IN MATERIALS

The group of Y4/5 children had been handling a collection of metal objects and the transcript begins with a reference back to comments made the day before in a similar group discussion. Unattributed comments are signalled with 'U':

Teacher: Do you remember, yesterday, Thomas said all of these would melt.
Ella: Some of them would melt.
Elinor: They'd all melt.

Bobak:	It depends what you're talking about.
U:	Not all of them.
Alice:	Some would take a long time to melt.
Elinor:	They would melt straight away, but other stuff would take longer to melt. In the end I don't know if they all would.
U:	Yeah, in the end.
Thomas:	This [painted object] might burn.
U:	In the end.
Bobak:	This [block] would crack, and the others would melt.
Teacher:	So why do you think that?
Bobak:	Because that's [the block] stronger.
Elinor:	I don't know; I think it would probably melt because . . .
Teacher:	How would it crack?
Thomas:	It would crack first and then melt.
Bobak:	Probably the heat would make it sort of disintegrate and expand, and disintegrate and burn. . .

At this point the teacher encouraged the group to clarify their use of words. This helped the children to come to a shared understanding of the phenomena they were discussing, and, incidentally, provided the prompt that led to a change of direction:

Teacher:	What does disintegrate mean?
Elinor:	It crumbles, sort of crumbles away and disappears.
Teacher:	What about expand?
U:	Get bigger.
Teacher:	Do things usually expand when you heat them up?
Alice:	Well, marshmallows do, if you put them on the fire and leave them . . . they sort of . . . because . . .
Elinor:	And they pop.
U:	And they sort of . . . a bit of it pops up and then all the pink stuff comes out.
Alice:	Exactly.
U:	Gungy.

U:	And it all goes really lush.
Bobak:	And then it goes all hard and it goes black ...
U:	It happened at her party. Simon left it by the fire.
U:	Yeah, it just dribbled ...
Alice:	And it expanded ... it went sort of bubble, bubble, bubble.

At this point Bobak linked the ideas about marshmallows to other previous experiences he had had related to cooking, probably at home:

Bobak:	Cakes expand ... if you put self-raising flour in them.
U:	Yeast in ...
Alice:	Bread expands with yeast.
Teacher:	How does that work I wonder?
Ella:	I don't know.
Bobak:	It just does. But I don't think it gets really, actually gets any bigger; it's just more air underneath, or inside it.
U:	It gets more air in it, yeah.

The yeast contribution signalled another change in direction, which, according to the next comment, confused Elinor and led to her combining the two threads of the conversation.

Elinor:	Yeah, like bread, you use more self-raising flour in that, so it all puffs up.
Ella:	Or yeast.
Alice:	If you use yeast it does actually grow a little bit.
Elinor:	Yeah, like in that story where it keeps growing and growing, you know.

The quality of the children's utterances in this discussion and the diverse ideas expressed are not a result of constant teacher intervention or questioning. The teacher's contribution was minimal. She did however, have a crucial role, valuing children's contributions by actively listening to them and allowing them to control the discussion's direction. She avoided any suggestion of wanting a 'right answer'. She had also created a classroom ethos which allowed the children to feel confident to share their ideas and talk openly.

This kind of atmosphere is not achieved overnight, nor can it be adopted suddenly during science work; it is an aspect of the classroom which needs to permeate all interactions between teacher and children. It was as a result of children having control, and feeling that their contributions were valued, that the dialogue in the case-study was productive and led to the children making links between one idea and another. The dialogue made several leaps, from metals to the shared experience of marshmallows (a change of direction that the teacher could not have made or even anticipated), from marshmallows to cakes and finally to bread and the role of yeast. We have here an example of children using language 'to make knowledge their own ... (by) ... putting old familiar experience into words in order to see new patterns in it and trying to make sense of new experience by finding a way of relating it to the old.' (Barnes, 1976).

The conversation provided the teacher with several insights into the children's existing ideas related to properties of materials. Some of these were insights which she could not have easily anticipated at the outset, for example Bobak's idea about air being the cause of cakes expanding when cooked. There is also evidence here of children exploring their ideas, as well as simply expressing them, through talk. Barnes (1976) identifies a considerable difference between exploratory talk and 'final draft', polished, talk that is for the teacher's benefit. Barnes noted the problems implicit in a teacher thinking of a pupil's language in terms of performance instead of in terms of learning. Children need time to reflect and reorganise their thoughts. Overemphasis on requiring immediate and 'polished' answers discourages such processes from occurring.

Other issues arise through consideration of this episode. In particular the way in which the half-formed and incomplete ideas of an individual might influence the ideas of others in the group. Teachers need to be aware of this and encourage children to evaluate the ideas of others and regard them as useful only if they can stand the challenge of being tested against experience or other 'tested' ideas. It is also important to recognise the significance of 'what happens next' in terms of a teacher encouraging children to develop their ideas. In the case of this group of children the teacher followed up the discussion by encouraging the group, with adult supervision, to explore what happens to a variety of materials, including some foods, when

54

heated. A later session in the food activities area was used to observe more closely changes to ingredients when baked. This led to an investigation using self-raising and plain flour to make small cakes.

The teacher involved above had taped her discussion with the children. The time required to transcribe a tape means that it is not normally practical to keep a record of group discussions in this way. However, selective use of a tape-recorder under either the teacher's or the children's control is possible. Some teachers leave a tape-recorder with a group and invite the children to turn it on to record something that they think is interesting: this could be a question, an observation, an explanation or an idea for testing out. Other teachers decide at which point in the discussion, perhaps at the review or concluding stage, the conversation requires recording.

Children's language can be a barrier, preventing teachers gaining an insight into their understanding. Teachers who expect children to 'mime' a provided answer gain little. Also suspect are words collected by the children from elsewhere. There is no guarantee that children understand the words they are using, however confident their usage might appear. In contrast some children's use of naive language might mask sophisticated understanding. This raises the question of when teachers should introduce children to specific scientific terminology. Brenda Presst (ASE, 1980) sums it up well:

> Words introduced too soon are part of the 'verbal wrapping paper' of science ... Many teachers say that children 'like' to use technical words even though their understanding of them is very limited. I would suggest that wrapping paper can be very gaudy and attractive but it still covers and obscures the contents of the parcel.

Some teachers use a *Science Word Dictionary* which is a large-format book which children use to enter their own words (e.g. 'twangy') and definitions (the feel of a string moving backwards and forwards very quickly). A word remains in the dictionary until a 'better' or more appropriate word (such as 'vibration') is invented or found.

Children's language is vital to their learning in science and talk is just as important as activity in the classroom. This will be discussed again in the context of restructuring ideas in Chapter 4.

c. Using floor-books

A practical and common strategy for collecting and recording children's elicited ideas is a floor-book. This is a large-format book (usually several sheets of A1 sugar paper folded in half) in which the teacher, or another adult helper, notes down the children's utterances during small-group or even whole-class discussions. An individual's name is written beside each utterance. Sometimes each child has a differently coloured felt pen and hands this to the teacher when he or she makes a contribution.

The benefits of this very public record are numerous. The children see their comments are valued: they are written down in their original form, not edited by the teacher. The teacher can ensure that all the children make a contribution and the children are made aware that everyone is involved. They are required to listen to, and value, other children's ideas. The act of writing down the comments slows the discussion. This could be considered a disadvantage but in fact allows the children that precious time to think mentioned earlier in the chapter. In this way it facilitates the structuring of ideas that is fundamental to elicitation. The record becomes something that both teacher and children can refer back to, either later in the discussion, when further exploration and investigation have been done, or at the point of reviewing and drawing conclusions. Some teachers maintain a floor-book throughout an activity; others use it to record ideas at the outset. A group's floor-book can remain with the group as they work and be added to when the teacher 'visits'. We will return to the sustained use of floor-books more fully in Chapter 5.

The following comments recorded in a floor-book being used with Y1 children provide an example of the sort of dialogue that can easily be noted by a teacher joining a group for a few minutes. The teacher's questions were also put in the floor-book. The children were discussing what would happen to various examples of litter if they were left on the window-sill. The teacher had just asked what would happen to the half-eaten apple:

Jonathan:	The apple will go brown.
Teacher:	Why?
Jonathan:	Because it wouldn't have enough water.
Robert:	It needs water to keep it alive.
Jonathan:	It can't be alive because it isn't an animal.
Robert:	OK, but it needs water to grow.
Teacher:	Will it grow?
Robert:	I think it will rot and smell.
Rachel:	It might grow.
Nicholas:	I think it will go dry and shrivel.
Anna:	It won't go dry in a plastic bag.
Teacher:	Why not?
Anna:	Because the air can't get in.
Thomas:	If we left it outside in the winter it would go frosty.
Nicholas:	It will go bad and we won't be able to eat it.
Rachel:	If you eat it when it is rotten you might get a big tummy ache because all the germs have got on it.

A floor-book offers the teacher an insight into the children's thinking similar to that provided by the transcribed tape analysed in the 'Changes in materials' case-study (p.50), but the evidence is collected more practically and other benefits gained. This particular floor-book, essentially recording the children's predictions and tentative hypotheses, was referred to after the apple pieces had been left a fortnight (unwatered, watered and sealed in a plastic bag) as the children reviewed their ideas. In the meantime the floor-book was on display for other children to refer to and as a means of encouraging parents to recognise the process aspects of science. Other examples of floor-books have previously been discussed by Ritchie (1991b; 1992). One of these is an example of a floor-book being used effectively during a whole-class discussion.

Word-spurs or key-words can be included in floor-books or produced as a separate poster or recorded in individual folders or books. They are a means of eliciting the use children are making of a certain key word. For example, during a discussion with Y2 children, recorded in a floor-book, one child used the word 'energy' to explain how a clockwork toy operated: 'There's a spring inside which winds up and gives it energy'. The teacher wrote 'Energy' in the centre of a new page of the floor-book and asked the rest of the small group if they had any ideas about energy. Comments made, such as, 'You eat food to get energy', 'Mum says I've got lots of energy', 'We switch off the lights to save energy', were written around the key word beside the contributors' names.

Web diagrams can be produced as part of a floor-book, or as posters, or on the board, as a result of brainstorming a topic or area of science with a small group or whole class (see Ritchie, 1991b). In this method of elicitation children are invited to contribute ideas in the broad area of a topic or theme. Any contribution made is noted and later discussed and organised into a more structured web. This later stage is difficult and is often done by the teacher and fed back to the children for comment. The knowledge that teachers have related to the content being covered may mean they can identify ways of grouping and combining contributions which will make organisation and management of the activities more practical and focused. However, it is important that, whenever feasible, all the original ideas are included. In this way, it is possible for children to play an active part in topic planning and at the same time gain ownership of the work.

Another advantage of a floor-book is that the teacher can use it to structure an adult helper's work with the children. Key questions at the top of each sheet can be a prompt for a non-teaching assistant, or a well-briefed parent, working with the children. Their role is to act as scribe and note down the children's responses which can be used by the teacher to inform the next stage of the children's work.

Many of these strategies, which require learners to expose their tentative and perhaps naive ideas, require sensitive handling by the teacher. The children need to share their ideas in a situation where they do not risk being ridiculed by their teacher or other children. Hesitancy can be overcome, particularly with older children who perhaps haven't previously been expected to share their ideas, by asking them to talk to a partner first and contribute a shared idea, or to write down their ideas on paper to give to the teacher more anonymously.

d. Using children's written and drawn outcomes

As children become more independent writers their written work can be a valuable source of evidence of existing ideas. This is only likely to happen, however, if they are encouraged to record their tentative ideas and explanations. The most common form of recording, done after an activity, is too often merely descriptive, telling a teacher little. More useful writing is that which is explanatory (see Chapter 5) and in which there is an attempt to clarify ideas. Harlen (1985) recognises the value of such outcomes:

> Children use their notebooks to express themselves, and to communicate; they are like mirrors. These notebooks help the teacher to know what the children have thought about, how they have thought about it, what they have observed, what they have been or still are interested in. Harlen (1985, p.99)

We earlier quoted a child's comment about the purpose of talk, which echoes, unwittingly, something E.M. Forster once said: 'How do I know what I think until I see what I write?'. For some children writing can be a useful way of organising thoughts and making sense of the wealth of experiences they are having. Chapter 5 deals with recording in more depth and at this stage we are only briefly highlighting the place of children's recording during the elicitation phase. The writing can be individual or collaborative; it can be a record of one child's or a group's ideas. The terms 'think-book' and 'science journal' have been used to describe this continuing record which gives the child much more control of what is written and when. The think-book can be similar in purpose to a floor-book if it is used to record a group's ideas. If it remains an individual record it is perhaps more appropriately thought of as a 'science journal'. Word-processing on computers has a useful role here since it allows children to get their ideas quickly onto paper and modify them easily. It can be particularly useful if a concept keyboard is available and the teacher constructs an overlay using the child's own words. The other important benefit of word-processors is that they allow children to write collaboratively and this can be an appropriate way of coming to a common view (see MAPE, 1989; Hemsley et al., 1991).

Other techniques for eliciting and retaining children's ideas or getting them to clarify their own, include mapping diagrams, flow diagrams and concept maps. Concept maps offer considerable potential for looking at the way children's ideas are linked together and examples will be discussed later in the book.

Children's drawn outcomes also express their existing ideas. The example below was produced by a six-year-old who was trying to show what happens when an inflated balloon is released. The series of drawings clearly reveal the ideas that air is something contained within the balloon, that air rushes out and causes the balloon to move, and that the motion of the balloon is random.

6. How do we encourage children to raise questions?

During orientation and elicitation it is important that children raise questions as well as make statements. The way a teacher encourages and deals with children's questions can have a crucial

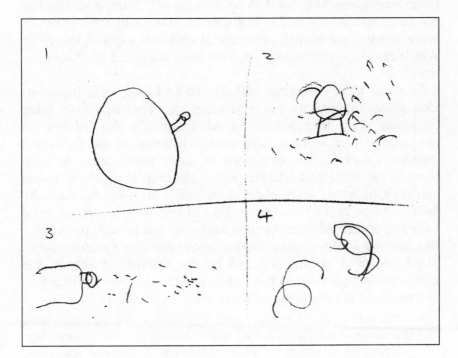

Figure 3.1

effect on the nature of the investigative work and the extent to which the children genuinely engage with an activity. There is a need to be more explicit than is sometimes the case about how important we consider children's questions to be. There is evidence that children who are bombarded with teachers' questions are less likely to raise their own. Children's questions have been discussed usefully by others (Harlen, 1992, p.116; Jelly, 1985, p.47) but it is perhaps worth reminding ourselves at this point what prolific question-raisers children are before they reach school. The nature of pre-school learning is markedly different from school learning in a number of significant ways. Tizard & Hughes (1984), in a fascinating study of thirty four-year-old girls from different social backgrounds, looked at pre-school learning and compared it with learning in nursery schools. They recorded the conversation of the young children at home with mothers and confessed to becoming increasingly impressed with the home as a learning environment and the young child as a learner. Pre-school learning is not systematic but is usually self-motivated, relevant and meaningful to the learner. Young children naturally test out their own ideas and ask lots of questions (Tizard and Hughes recorded an average of 26 questions an hour, a quarter of which were 'why?' questions!). Pre-school children explore things in which they are interested, in their own way and in their own time.

At home most dialogues with Tizard and Hughes's four-year-olds were initiated by the individual children; in school most dialogues were initiated by an adult, usually the teacher. In the dialogues at home adults usually listened to the children's questions and then commented or gave information to help them clarify their ideas. In school the children's responses to the teacher's question were often short and were only occasionally followed up. There is a picture here of children, in school, who have lost control of their learning and with that loss of control also the desire or motivation to find out about the world around them. The number of questions raised by the children in school was dramatically less than in the home and there were no instances of persistent questioning, as there were in the home.

> In school ... the richness, depth and variety which characterised the home conversations was sadly missing ... the questioning, puzzling child which we were so taken with at home was gone. (Tizard and Hughes, 1984.)

There may, of course, be other factors at work here since children reaching school age are undergoing other changes such as rapid growth, increasing language competence and other forms of physical and cognitive development. The exact nature of this development is too complex to be dealt with adequately in this book, but, despite these reservations, there do seem to be some factors in the findings that deserve teachers' attention, paricularly in the light of other research in classrooms. The ORACLE study (Galton et al., 1980) provides a wealth of evidence about the teacher's role and classroom talk. Their study found that in most classrooms someone was talking for two thirds of the time and, of that talk, about two thirds was done by the teacher. The vast majority of questions were posed by the teacher and one third of these questions related to task supervision. Only five per cent were open questions related to work the children were doing.

However, before becoming too dispirited about such schools let us consider how the inherently formal context of the classroom might allow children to develop their 'homely' curiosity and the desire to raise questions, which we regard as important aspects of elicitation. Raising questions helps children clarify what it is they already think and know and what it is they would like to find out more about. The stimulation provided by the environment in which the children work is obviously important and the provision of interesting and relevant artefacts, materials and experiences can play an important part in encouraging question raising. The inclusion of the novel and unexpected can be particularly successful in engaging children as an important first step to question-raising.

Some teachers have devised practical strategies for supporting children in asking their own questions. Ann Orchard, a Y2 teacher in a Bristol school, whose case-study 'Minibeasts' features in Chapters 4 and 5, regularly brainstorms with the children for questions about a topic or theme, contributes her own, and makes explicit use of the questions (Ritchie, 1991b). Her children's skills in question-raising have been built up systematically using a variety of contexts, including question-and-answer games and computer programs such as 'Sorting Game' and 'Branch'. (See illustrations in Chapter 5). At the beginning of the year she found that the children, rather than formulating questions, were more often making statements which implied them. Their skills improved and by the summer term, with a topic on Minibeasts, they were raising questions confidently. The children were encouraged to sort their own questions into categories of their own choosing. The topic raised many questions which were divided into those that could be answered by looking (Has it got a shell?), by watching (Does it fly?), by testing (Do snails prefer wet or dry?), by looking in books (Do all spiders make webs?) and those that could not be answered (How long is a snail's birthday?). Some questions, such as, 'What do ladybirds eat?' the children decided could be answered by several means (watching, testing or reading books). After the grouping and further discussion, all of which helped the children understand the nature of their own questions, and provided the teacher with insight into their existing ideas, the children selected questions from 'those that could be tested' as the basis of investigations. One of these investigations is featured in Chapter 4.

The extent to which children are raising questions, but not formulating them as questions, is significant because a teacher alert to this can help children rephrase their statements appropriately. Jelly, (1985, p.53) provides sound advice on how to recognise the type of questions children are raising and how to encourage 'productive questions' which, in her terms, 'stimulate productive activity'.

The effective teacher recognises the importance of children's own questions as the means by which exploration can become investigation and as another vital source of evidence of children's existing ideas and ways of behaving scientifically.

7. What influences a child's ideas about the world?

The significance to subsequent learning of the ideas children bring to school, makes it worth considering the origins of these ideas and the influences upon them. It is evident that many of these ideas do not match accepted scientific thinking and therefore a teacher's attempts to help the child develop more scientifically acceptable understanding may be helped by an awareness of these influences. In the context of elicitation, such an awareness should inform the nature of the questions a teacher asks or the nature of the activities offered. In this section we will explore further the differences between classroom learning, which we will refer to as 'formal', and the 'informal' learning that usually happens outside the classroom and school. It is important to state at this point that the following discussion ventures into the complex area of cognitive development. The perspective is offered tentatively with the sole intention of highlighting aspects considered relevant to a constructivist approach. The exact means by which ideas develop in the child's mind is perhaps of less significance than a recognition of the influences on that development and a recognition that an active process is involved. The conceptual framework of a young child is a dynamic, flexible and incomplete structure.

Children have many direct experiences that inform the cognitive models of the world they develop. It is from these experiences that initial concepts begin to form. For example, if we are looking at how ideas about heat (an energy form) and temperature (a measurement of hotness and coldness), develop, then a vast number and range of first-hand experiences will have played a part. Very young children experience the difference between hot and cold surroundings and obviously sense the difference between the feel of an ice-cream and a hot-water bottle. These sensory experiences and more extreme ones, like touching a hot kettle or iron, frozen food or snow, are organised in the child's mind to develop a concept of hot and cold. Some direct experiences may offer evidence that conflicts with 'first thoughts'; for example, the cold water from the tap feels 'warm' to freezing cold hands. Children have to make sense of such experiences in their own terms. Their mental picture of the world, constructed as a result of their experience, will include intuitive features. In other words, children are likely to connect ideas and hold meanings for words which are based on intuition and guess-work since their experience will be limited. Many of these links and ways of organising individual concepts will be implicit in the way a child acts and the need may not have arisen for these links to have been clarified or articulated.

Other experiences that are not direct, but can also be included in our account of informal learning, can also influence the construction of ideas. A child may well have heard adults saying, 'Shut the door and don't let the cold in' or 'Come in, or you'll catch cold', or played with toys described as 'Hot wheels'. These and other informal experiences may contribute to the child's model and may create or reinforce alternative ideas that do not match accepted scientific understanding. Harlen (1985) refers to these informal influences as 'ready-made' ideas that are offered the child. In her terms, these can be considered as 'free-floating' ideas which become part of the child's cognitive model but are less firmly linked into the overall structure than other concepts, established through direct experience, until they themselves are tested and found to be supported by further evidence. It is at this point that they become the child's own ideas. This may happen when, for example, the child who has started to think of 'cold' as something that is substantive, that can travel, opens a refrigerator and feels the 'cold'. To the child this may be evidence to support the alternative idea suggested by a parent's use of language. The alternative idea that cold is substantive may become a firmly held belief before the child reaches school.

Before the child comes to school parents are also likely to have set up activities with more obvious learning intentions for their children. A young child cooking with his or her parent and having a conversation about what will happen when the ingredients are cooked will be gaining information and valuable experiences that will contribute to the cognitive map building up about heat. The same child who later plays an imaginative cooking game and chooses something to use as an 'oven glove' is constructing new ideas, or consolidating early ideas, about insulation. Because parents and their children are emotionally close and share life, with a common history, the relationship is particularly conducive to relevant learning. The learning that occurs therefore takes place in a context of considerable meaning to the child. It is, perhaps, for this reason that ideas resulting from experiences at home can be firmly held and resistant to change. Similarly, older siblings can have an influence on the young learner. An eight-year-old boy, discussing dissolving with a teacher, was absolutely sure that the cup would eventually be dissolved by the water in it, 'because my brother told me'. All these experiences, be they direct, informal or specifically organised, influence the child's understanding of the world. It is hardly surprising that this mixture of experiences that children have before, and when they reach, school age, leads to partly-formed and scientifically unacceptable ideas. Indeed, this process continues throughout life! However, in some respects the young child has already learnt to behave scientifically. Tizard and Hughes (1984) described their sample as follows:

Armed only with their curiosity, logic and persistence, the children tackled the task of making sense of a world they imperfectly understood. Because of their inexperience they could rule out few inferences or explanations: almost everything had to be treated as possible until shown to be otherwise'.

Viewed in this way the child can be seen as having something in common with 'real' scientists. A scientist who was about to explore an unvisited area of jungle said in a radio interview:

> We go armed only with our senses, fully alert, and with whatever experience we can manage to bring to bear on what we find.'

When a child reaches school, learning becomes more systematic and under a teacher's control. The autonomy of learning, available to the young child, may be lost unless teachers are prepared to foster it. For children, school provides a new set of social, cultural and ideological factors that affect the development of ideas (Pollard, 1985). If school learning is to lead to the child modifying or replacing existing ideas then the new ideas provided must be recognised as more useful than existing ideas for offering explanations. Ideas about heat, introduced in a classroom context, need to challenge the child's existing ideas which may, for example, include a concept of 'cold' being something substantive. Unless this existing idea is made explicit, through elicitation, it is quite possible that experiences offered in the school context will be interpreted by the children as reinforcing their alternative idea(s). The idea a child takes away from a learning experience may not be the one anticipated by the teacher (Osborne and Freyberg, 1985, p.86).

Once school (formal) learning begins, the extent to which it can influence a learner's existing ideas will, mainly, be a result of the skills of the teacher. Some ideas may be introduced through direct instruction and be useful to the learner and therefore readily accepted. The children who arrive in school with certain ideas about heat and temperature may find themselves instructed in the use of a thermometer and this may lead to the active reconstruction of their previous ideas; temperature becomes measurable and an understanding of temperature being a continuum is clarified.

Activities related to 'keeping things warm' and 'insulation' may be tackled in a systematic and structured way. Through appropriate teacher support, as we will explore in more detail in the next chapter, the children can be encouraged to question their existing ideas and modify them appropriately. For example, children's explanations for why polystyrene feels warm are discussed in Harlen (1985). Some stated that it must have a source of heat inside, perhaps drawing on previous experiences with hot water bottles. Older children were able to suggest tests to find out whether this is true. However, they became confused when the polystyrene did not appear to feel cold even when it had been placed in a refrigerator to see if it would cool. Only relating this experience to the fact that woollen gloves don't feel cold helped them make sense of this experience. To enable children to restructure their existing ideas, as we will discuss in Chapter 4, new ideas need to be: understood by them; believable and supported by evidence; apply consistently in a variety of situations; be useful, especially in terms of problem solving; explain phenomena more satisfactorily to the child than their existing ideas.

Of course, direct and informal experiences outside school continue to play an important part in the child's life and indeed make a contribution to learning that may easily be underestimated by the busy teacher. Watching adult television programmes may provide children with experiences that help them collect scientific words (like thermodynamics) for later display in a formal school setting. The experience of riding a bicycle on a cold day and discovering the metal parts feel colder than the plastic handlebar grips may reinforce ideas about cold being quantitative and substantive: 'There is more cold coming from the shiny bit'.

Interestingly, there is considerable evidence, amongst children and adults in different parts of the country and indeed in different countries, of common alternative ideas. The fact that similar ideas are identified in different children is of some consolation to teachers who can develop an awareness of some of the likely ideas children bring to the school situation. For example, the idea that cold is something that can 'flow' from one place to another is a widely held alternative idea amongst both children and adults. The implications of this are considered in the next section.

8. What do we know about common alternative ideas?

Piaget, an early constructivist, was one of the first to recognise common patterns in the naive ideas young children hold.

However, it is over the last twenty years that researchers and teachers have explored these ideas in all age ranges and across all areas of scientific content. During the seventies and early eighties, the research tended to focus on secondary and, in some cases, tertiary students. These findings are reviewed by Osborne and Freyberg (1985), Driver and Erickson (1983) and Gilbert and Watts (1983). Some were simply attempts to analyse learners' existing ideas but others attempted to offer ways of dealing with these existing ideas. A variety of approaches, all based on a constructivist perspective, were articulated. Common to all of these was the recognition of the need to elicit children's existing ideas and base any teaching decisions on a knowledge of them.

A major project, in England, was the Children's Learning in Science (CLIS) Project, directed by Rosalind Driver at Leeds University. This project produced reports of research findings into secondary pupils' understanding of several areas of science (CLIS, 1984-1991). These were then followed by classroom materials to support secondary teachers in adopting the constructivist approach advocated by the team (Scott, 1987). INSET materials were also produced to raise teachers' awareness of the nature of children's existing ideas. The CLIS researchers found, for example, that thirty per cent of sixteen-year-old pupils hold the alternative idea that cold is substantive and can travel. This, despite the fact that all of the children had had five years of formal science in secondary schools which had included conventional teaching about heat. The conclusion to be drawn from these findings was that school science was not having the effect on pupils' understanding that teachers anticipated. Children were holding on to their intuitive ideas despite the best endeavours of science teachers.

There was also evidence that these ideas were established earlier rather than later and therefore the implications for primary teachers were considerable. This project was widely disseminated to secondary science teachers and began to influence primary science through, for example, the work of primary advisory teachers who had themselves been introduced to a constructivist approach through CLIS. The CLIS team have subsequently extended their brief to cover the full 5 – 16 range.

However, more extensive work in the primary field has resulted from the Science Processes and Concept Exploration (SPACE) Project based at King's College and Liverpool University and directed by Paul Black and Wynne Harlen. This is a classroom-based research project which aims to establish the ideas primary school children have in particular areas of science and explore how these existing ideas might be modified. To date, it has produced extremely useful reports covering electricity; evaporation and condensation; everyday changes in non-living materials; forces and their effect on movement; growth; light; living things' sensitivity to their environment; sound (SPACE, 1990-92). Each of these reports documents and analyses the ideas of primary children recorded by their classroom teachers, who had been trained by the project team. These ideas were elicited after an orientation period, which involved specified exploratory activities, and again after teacher-interventions that were designed, by the project team and teacher, to modify the children's ideas. The elicitation strategies used included pupil log-books (pictorial and written), structured writing and drawing (in response to particular questions), picture completion activities (children were asked to add to the relevant points in a given picture) and individual discussion. These reports provide the most comprehensive picture yet of the unorthodox ideas which children hold and provide practical ways of challenging them. Together they provide clear evidence that primary children from the age of five have explanations for phenomena and that these explanations often fit into some common pattern.

It is not possible to discuss, in this book, the nature of all of these alternative ideas although you will find examples evident in many case-studies. However, as an indication, we offer some of the common ideas found in two areas of science. There is, of course, a danger in simplifying the nature of alternative ideas to single statements since an individual's existing ideas are likely to be more complex than the single statement suggests. The simplification also glosses over the nature of the restructuring that is required – it may be a simple reorganisation of existing concepts that is needed or it may require a significant conceptual change which will be far more demanding for both learner and teacher. This problem is discussed by Carey (1989) and will be explored in the next chapter. However, despite these limitations, it is important for teachers to know more about the kinds of alternative ideas their children may hold.

Common alternative ideas about electric circuits include:

(a) Electricity goes down one wire, gets used up at the bulb and the other wire is a 'dead' wire;
(b) Electricity goes down both wires and 'clashes' in the bulb;
(c) Electricity goes down one wire, some gets used up in the bulb and less comes back through the return wire.

Common alternative ideas about evaporation from a container include:

(a) The water leaks away;
(b) The water is drunk (usually at night or when no-one is looking) by a small animal;
(c) The sun sucks it up (as water);
(d) It changes into air;
(e) It disappears.

Without an awareness of the likely ideas children may hold it is possible that certain unexpected ideas (such as the role of small creatures in the process of evaporation) will be retained by the child even though the teacher may think otherwise. Children seem to be very good at giving teachers the impression of acceptance of a teacher-introduced idea, whilst perhaps holding on, stubbornly, to their own naive, but workable alternative. This seems especially likely, according to research findings, when it comes to explaining similar phenomena in other contexts. The teacher who identifies alternative ideas in their children needs to find ways of challenging them. It is possible that the existing ideas have had adequate personal explanatory power for the individual and will be replaced only by ones with more explanatory potential, that is equally personally satisfying. The emotional attachment children, and adults, may have for particular personal alternative ideas is of significance. A young child who is constructing an understanding of living processes may well have emotional reasons for holding on to ideas of immortality where his or her pet is concerned.

Evidence has also been found that, not surprisingly, many primary teachers, in common with many other adults, hold views about the world which do not match accepted scientific thinking. The research of the Primary School Teachers and Science (PSTS) Project, based at Oxford University (PSTS, 1988-91) indicates that many of these common ideas held by teachers are similar to those held by children. This has some disturbing implications. How can primary teachers assess ideas that they themselves do not understand or decide on appropriate next steps for a learner towards accepted scientific understanding?

It is perhaps appropriate to identify different kinds of scientific understanding and their relationship (based on ideas from Gilbert, Watts and Osborne, 1985). Scientists' science can be regarded as the accepted understanding of phenomena tentatively shared by the community of scientists. A subset and simplified version of this is chosen by curriculum planners and used as the basis for curriculum materials and the National Curriculum. Each teacher and child also has his/her own unique set of scientific ideas, including ideas which do not match with those of the scientists' science or curriculum science. These sets of ideas can be considered as teachers' science and children's science. The outcome of learning science in school should be a development of children's science to a version which more closely matches with curriculum science. This new set of ideas, unique to individuals, including some of their original ideas and some new ones, can be seen as pupils' science.

To facilitate a child's learning in these terms teachers need to recognise the inadequacies and incomplete nature of their own 'teachers' science'; if teachers are to decide how to develop the children's existing ideas so that they construct an understanding of the world around them which more closely matches accepted scientific ideas and theories, it is clearly necessary for them to improve their own knowledge base in the area of science. This issue will be addressed in Chapter 8 when we explore teachers' professional development. The PSTS team have published materials, based on the research and an espoused constructivist approach, designed to help teachers improve their knowledge and understanding of science. This aspect of primary teachers' professional development is also the focus of DES-funded courses that have run in many parts of the country since 1989. The National Curriculum requirements have highlighted the need for primary teachers to have an understanding of science not hitherto needed.

10. Does elicitation help me with assessment?

In some respects the aim of elicitation can be regarded as part of formative assessment. If the aim of assessment is to gain insight into children's learning in order to decide on the next appropriate step, then elicitation is fulfilling that aim. However, as we will discuss later, it is also a form of self-assessment, in that it is through elicitation that the learners become aware of their own existing ideas and the extent to which those existing ideas have adequate explanatory power. Within the constructivist model that is being advocated throughout this book, assessment and teaching are inextricably linked and although Chapter 6 focuses on aspects of assessment it will be a theme that permeates throughout.

11. Summary

Elicitation is, as we have seen, about helping children to find out and clarify what they think. It is usually during exploratory, often unstructured, work that children can best be helped to discover what they already know. Not only do we need to help them express, in their own terms, what they know but also to encourage them to consider why they hold these ideas. They should be invited to consider other possibilities. The recognition that others hold different ideas is a crucial part of elicitation and individuals should be encouraged to reflect on how this might happen. In this way, learners are made aware of the tentative nature of their own and other people's ideas, including those of scientists. Understanding the tentativeness of ideas is an important step in becoming open to new possibilities and being prepared to change existing ideas.

In engaging in exploratory work children will inevitably be involved in practical activity, using scientific and more generic skills to collect and organise information and to raise questions. The skills will include: observing, using secondary sources, discussing, classifying, reporting, explaining, finding patterns, predicting and hypothesising. The teacher will also need certain skills, including active listening and responsive questioning. Asking the right question at the right time is perhaps more easily said than done and it may be that it is often better not to ask a question at all! Teachers need to develop management skills to facilitate elicitation. They will need to manage classes in order to provide opportunities to talk on a one-to-one basis, work with small groups and handle class discussions sensitively. Children need to listen to, and discuss, each other's ideas and need to be helped to select what is relevant from all that they hear.

In terms of providing teachers with useful insights into children's existing ideas, elicitation can take anything from a few minutes to several weeks. However, the insight gained is of value only if it can be used constructively by the teacher to take the child forward to an understanding that better corresponds to conventional scientific thinking. How this might be achieved is the theme of the next chapter.

CHAPTER 4
Restructuring and Review

1. Introduction

> According to the constructivist model, all knowledge is simply conclusions drawn from experience (whether direct or second hand). As such, all knowledge should remain provisional because new experiences may require a restructuring of existing understanding, for example, when a child who knows that red balls bounce better than blue ones comes across a particularly bouncy blue one or when physicists discover that an atomic explanation of matter cannot adequately account for their observations'. (Parker-Rees, Thyer, and Ollerenshaw, 1991, p.7)

This chapter is about identifying where children's thinking has got to at a particular moment and how to challenge their ideas in order that the learning process shall continue – in other words how to activate the restructuring process after elicitation. To do this, much reference will be made to case-studies in order to discuss the dangers of making careless assumptions about children's ideas and to examine the need to help children design investigations for themselves and learn how to recognise testable questions. The case-studies, therefore, help in the examination of ways of enabling children to *trust their own ideas, respect evidence* with the help of *reviewing procedures* that they have undertaken and, as a result, *draw conclusions* to assist them in finding *changed explanations* for what they have understood. Since we will shortly be reading children's utterances recorded verbatim, it will be wise, first, to make some further observations about children's use of language. After all, everything depends on our understanding it.

2. Language

> We cannot control what people think, therefore we must hear it
> and work with it and relate teaching to their ideas. (Osborne and
> Freyberg, 1985)

Language is an exploration of thought. We can reflect upon our
thoughts through language − we can clarify them, compare them
and own them. As we have seen in earlier chapters language is
as much a part of the action in the classroom as is investigating
and exploring. It is the means by which children are helped to
come to an understanding of ideas. Language allows them to
internalise and carry with them ideas from which they can form
theories. It is for all of us significant to realise that what we *think*
is as important as what we *know* and that language is our means
of explaining the links between the two.

Language can be the means by which mere encounters become
learning experiences; it is socially constructed and individually
understood. The language of science includes many every day
words with specific meanings and a whole vocabulary less commonly used. Scientific concepts are often described or explained
with the help of metaphoric or analogous models. Children's
thinking is generally represented in what they say and in speech
patterns that become more complex with maturity. However, the
difficulty for the would-be interpreter of ideas is the smoke screen
of sophisticated and scientific language. Not all understanding is
as it sounds.

> Learning of this (scientific) kind may never progress beyond
> manual skills accompanied by slippery intuitions unless the
> learners themselves have an opportunity to go back over such
> experience and represent it to themselves. (Barnes, 1976)

It is precisely what the individual does with encounters which
determines whether events are 'experience' or 'learning' or
neither. Reflecting on encounters ensures that learning takes
place. Kelly (Britton, 1972, p.17) describes this reflection as
the construing of events. Learning is not determined by the
succeeding events themselves:

> It is the successive construing and reconstruing of what happens,
> as it happens, that enriches the experience of life.

For children to reflect upon encounters they need time as well as encouragement from the teacher to explore ideas through talking. This is another reason for heeding Barnes's warning against a teacher viewing language in terms of performance instead of in terms of learning.

Teachers often want children to 'perform' an answer, as if the spoken answer is the end of a process – the outcome, which can be checked for accuracy or correctness as the words emerge. To hear talking as an end-product in this way is to ignore its vital role as part of a process – the process of absorbing new experiences and making sense of them in the light of previous experiences. Children who are confident enough to think aloud will often contradict themselves, posit objections to what they themselves have just said – and perhaps omit to say at the end just where their thinking has got to. Some probing may be necessary to find out. Teachers who realise that talking is part of the learning process will allow time for children to reorganise their thoughts. The following case-study illustrates the point.

A group of children was watching as water was heated in a transparent container. This event was part of work on materials and the states of matter. The process of heating water was one that the teacher wanted them to think about. In this case-study an elicitation phase leads to restructuring of the ideas.

CASE-STUDY: HEATING WATER

A group of three Year 6 children, David, Tony and Rebecca, were asked to observe a jar of water as it was brought to the boil and then attempt to find explanations for what they thought was happening. The teacher was Tony Phillips of Chester Park School, Bristol.

David: There's *air*-bubbles in it.
Tony: There's a couple of *air*-bubbles on the top.
David: It looks like it's moving.
Rebecca: The *air*-bubbles are beginning to rise.
Tony: The pressure of the heat is making the bubbles rise.
(Temperature taken – 50 degrees C)
David: It's starting to evaporate.
The steam's on the side.
Rebecca: The *air*-bubbles are everywhere now.
Tony: It should be hot, smoke's coming from it.

76

David:	That's not smoke, it's steam.
	(Temperature taken – 79 degrees C)
David:	The *air*-bubbles are going up faster now.
Rebecca:	Yeah, and they're bigger.
	(Temperature taken – 97 degrees C)
David:	The bubbles are bubbling up really fast now and they're massive.
Tony:	The pressure must be really high now.
David:	You mean hot.
	(Temperature taken – 100 degrees C)
Tony:	I never knew there were so many air-bubbles in water.
David:	I suppose the heat's generating them.
Rebecca:	There's nothing on the bottom to make the bubbles. It's evaporating.
David:	The condensation is running down again.
Tony:	The water is full of pure air.
	(Temperature taken – 100 degrees C)
Tony:	The water level's gone down again.
	I wonder if water is just full of air, like fish have air from the sea.
David:	No, when you boil water to a certain extent it changes to steam.
	(Temperature taken – 100 degrees C)

At this point, the hotplate was turned off.

David:	It's slowing down now.
	The bubbles aren't as big.
Tony:	They're still going up fast.
Rebecca:	The temperature will go down now.
David:	It will stay high because it's still steaming.
	(Temperature taken – 97 degrees C)
David:	The bubbles have become fewer – there's not as many and you can see the smaller ones.
Tony:	It's nearly evaporated to 200 (m.l.)
	(Temperature taken – 94 degrees C)
David:	It's not steaming as much.
	There's not as many bubbles.
	(Temperature taken – 90 degrees C)
David:	The water turns into steam.
Teacher:	What were the bubbles?

Tony: Air – well, water.
Teacher: How can you have bubbles of water in water?
David: The water got hot and evaporated in the water. It couldn't go up on its own so it formed a bubble and joined other ones.
           The bubbles burst at the top and became steam.
Teacher: So what do you think the bubbles were then?
Rebecca: The bubbles were steam.

The children's conversation was a good example of thinking aloud and the way that children really working together restructured from their initial idea that the bubbles in the water were air to the view that they were steam. Their open discussion was again the result of a teacher who encouraged and valued their thinking and, on that occasion, intervened only to help the children draw a conclusion from their observations.

Understanding what children are trying to do when they are talking requires listening teachers, not talking teachers. For children to verbalise experience during and after an event, the help of at least one other person is usually required. 'Their own (the pupils') direct experience is blended with the teacher's offering of generalisations and conceptualisations'. (Torbe, 1986) The two meet as the pupil reorganises the information to understand it in his or her own way. When a group of children is genuinely working co-operatively the dimensions by which the individual can 'reconstrue' meaning are increased. Social interaction includes the wish to communicate meaning, the asking and answering of questions and the wish to involve others. All of these play a dynamic part in the construction of knowledge for the individual. The social and learning functions of language therefore work simultaneously.

The language used by the teacher is important. Teachers who use 'scientific' language or forms of words unfamiliar to the children can create a barrier to communication. Children can be placed at a disadvantage because they are unable to reply in the same terms. They may keep quiet, unwilling to look foolish or be wrong. A teacher may also lose confidence during an exchange with children when the gulf between them becomes apparent. A teacher may be insecure about his or her own understanding of the area of science and be unable to diagnose the children's ideas. Each may be experiencing equal difficulty: the teacher in interpreting the children's meaning and the children in making sense of the teacher's. This situation, according to Osborne and Freyberg, has resulted in teachers becoming nervous of straying from the planned lesson, unable to incorporate the children's ideas. While the teachers return to the comfort of their own language and framework, the children return to the insecurity of silent incomprehension.

Metaphors and analogies

Metaphors and analogies are used by children and teachers as well as scientists, to help explain phenomena. In the following comment, a Y3 child is using an analogy to explain his ideas about a circuit: 'It's like me and Thomas going through a tunnel and making a motor work and then running back through another tunnel and running back round again and again'. This provides a excellent explanation, in some respects, of an electric current and helps the child appreciate current does not get used up in the motor, but energy, carried by the current, is used to drive the motor. This kind of explanation gives the teacher more information than one in which the children simply bark the correct words without giving any clues as to how they understand them.

Sometimes teachers introduce metaphors to the children, and these can help children make sense of their experiences. The danger is that the teacher's analogy or metaphor may have little meaning for the child. It may make no sense at all if the children's framework for explaining is different from the teacher's. In consequence it is important to venture warily with offering metaphors. There is also the risk that the teacher's metaphor can actually foster ideas that are scientifically inappropriate. There is also a possibility that what the child understands from the teacher's metaphor reinforces some of the alternative ideas already established. Teachers who suggest to children that water 'has a skin' may be encouraging alternative ideas about the nature of surface tension. Children can gain much more from being encouraged to think of their own metaphors or similes (Ollerenshaw, 1989). Whereas adult-generated metaphors like 'skin' may easily be interpreted as facts, the children's own words will be known to be inventions to explain things.

However, used sensitively the metaphor or analogy can help to make a new concept intelligible. According to Gentner (1983), 'Analogies are of pivotal importance in conceptual change learning, in that they may help to structure existing memory and prepare it for new information'. Metaphors are valuable for opening up new possibilities, new ways of looking at things. One seven-year-old, David, like his peers, had been studying lichen on a piece of bank. The other children drew careful pictures and offered precise description of colour and shape: 'Pale green changing into dark green. Small and large cracks. Sort of leaves but small and crinkled.' David's analogy compared the lichen-covered bank with a wooded valley: 'There is like a river with lots of streams running into it. There are leafy trees up the valley with different coloured leaves. The river runs into a small dark lake.' The details David described mysteriously offered a more illustrative record of his observations than the more mechanical responses of the other children and are likely to be remembered more clearly and for a longer time.

It is obvious that the teacher's interpretation of the children's ideas is fundamental to the effective management of what follows. Much of that interpretation will be based on what children say. For children, too, what they say will influence the way they formulate and develop concepts. The teacher, then, will need to be aware of the way children use language to communicate their ideas and, at the same time, be aware of how children use language in the construction of learning.

3. Restructuring

In the restructuring phase of activity the teacher has to interpret children's ideas and questions in the light of the intended learning goals. Whether the activities that follow the exploration phase are purely illustrative or investigative or a mixture of both will depend upon the concepts involved, but in either case the children are likely to need to restructure their existing ideas. Children's alternative ideas are rarely illogical – for this reason they should not be dismissed as 'wrong' or 'immature' where they differ from a conventional scientific view. It has been recognised that children's existing ideas, learnt from everyday experiences of the world around them, are the ones they use to explain and interpret new experience. These personal understandings are powerful and resistant to change. It is with difficulty that people give up the security of their own manageable ideas for the insecurity of undertaking a new matching of evidence with understanding and the risks of having to trust new concepts. For the current scientific view to be accepted into individuals' frameworks those individuals must first have a clear understanding of the way their existing alternative ideas are pieced together. Knowing what we think and believe is a necessary step in the process of modification and change. When we ignore or deny our own ideas and struggle to accept those of others the task of learning becomes doubly difficult.

If children are to develop a respect for evidence and a willingness to challenge assumptions they will need to practise designing and undertaking investigation based on their own ideas. The restructuring of children's existing concepts may occur in a gradual and cumulative way or it may occur quite suddenly. For the purposes of helping children, planning must take account of such differences in pace. Often the focus of classwork is on brief illustrative activities, in the hope that the children's realisations will be dramatic. These snapshots can be useful provided they do not take the place of investigations which may provide a better context for conceptual development. It should also be remembered that brief encounters leave little opportunity to revisit ideas.

This restructuring phase of activity is concerned with designing investigations and with the way in which a teacher can help children to modify their thinking. Making decisions about development work with children must be based on sound evidence of their thinking. Chapters One and Two have already dealt with ways of eliciting children's ideas. The next case-study here serves to illustrate the danger of making assumptions about children's understanding based on first impressions and limited evidence. In fact the sequence reveals how the teachers involved unravelled the children's mixture of ideas about shadows and the strategies they employed to deal with them. In many ways it is a salutary tale. It was only the teachers' deliberate intention to react to the children's ideas rather than the knowledge to be taught that led to constructive intervention.

This work was carried out with five seven-year-olds in a primary school. Two teachers were involved. One collected data while the other worked with the children. The analysis and evaluative comments were as a result of both teachers working on the data they collected. The teachers, Neil Tuttiett of Mary Elton Primary School, Clevedon and Jennifer Allmand of Walliscote Primary School, Weston-Super-Mare, describe the work below:

CASE-STUDY: SHADOWS

We had planned work on shadows, assuming the children would already have had previous experiences that would have helped them form some ideas about the nature of shadows. The session began inside but the group soon moved to exploratory activities in the playground. All the pupils were able to observe shadows, even though it was a rather dull day.

T = Teacher; P = Pupil
T: Is it sunny today?
P1:   No.
T: Can you make a shadow?
P1:   Yes, see here's a shadow on the table. (P1 holds hand close to the table).
T: That's good, can you make it move?
P1:   Yes. (P1 moves hand slowly).
T: Let's go outside and see if we can make shadows. We need sun.
P2:   Here's a little clown here (P2 holds hand close to the ground).
T: Do you have to hold your hand close to the ground to make a shadow?
P2:   Yes, it's here.

After further unstructured exploratory activity we felt quite confident as they went back into the classroom that the children understood that the light originated with the sun and was being blocked to form a shadow.

We tested our assumption, back in the classroom, by asking, 'Can you draw a picture of yourself, your shadow and what we need to make shadows?' Stephanie drew a picture of the sun on the left and the shadow on the right. However, she drew her shadow separate from herself and with the head at her feet. She also drew eyes on her shadow. At this stage we did not pick up on this but noted that the order was correct but the orientation was wrong. Richard (P1) then made an interesting comment to the group:

P1:   When I come to school my shadow is small and when I go home it is big.
T: Why are you drawing the sun?
P3:   To make shadows.
T: How?
P3:   It hits you.
T: I don't understand, does it give you a smack?
P3:   Yes, it hits me here (points to chest) and comes out here behind.
T: Where is your shadow and what colour have you drawn on it? (referring to P4's picture)
P4:   It's red.

We are not certain how this came about or whether the children were having difficulty with recording or that they were confused by the properties of shadows. There seemed to be a vast difference in the understanding of shadows. Richard knew that they changed length, Amanda (P4) drew them red! We began to question our assumptions about the children's understanding.

We decided to move on to the next activity which was to make shadows using a torch and various pieces of constructional equipment. As soon as the children started using the torches I asked if they could make a shadow. The torch was shone onto the ceiling forming a pool of light.

T: Is that a shadow?
P4:   Yes.
T: What is the difference between that shadow and your 'hand' shadow?
P4:   The bulb has made the one on the ceiling.
T: Can you make a dark shadow on the ceiling?
P4:   No.

Everyone in the group was calling the pool of light a shadow. We did not challenge the view at this time, preferring simply to make the observation that the children were using the term shadow incorrectly. After several attempts at different lines of open questions to promote observation we were left with a group of children that appeared to know how to make shadows outside, some knew that light had to be blocked and yet all were calling light, 'shadows'.

T: What have you been doing?
P5:   Making shadows.
T: How do you make them?
P5:   We went outside.
T: What made the shadows?
P5:   It was the sun.
T: Was it sunny outside?
P5:   No, but we still made a shadow.
T: Have you made any other shadows?
P3:   Yes we shone the torch on the wall and moved it around.
T: How do you make a shadow?
P1:   You put your hand up here and then the light can't get through it so it makes a black mark.

In the next session we decided to give the children more experience of light being blocked to form shadows. We hoped to modify their understanding of the term shadow. We returned to the playground with various objects to make shadows. The children held each object in turn to see if it would have a shadow. It was almost as if they believed they would find one which didn't make a shadow. After this we went into the classroom where we had set up a photo-floodlight and a screen on which the children could make excellent shadows. It was at this point that we realised the difficulty language can present in the understanding of concepts. We asked the children to predict which of the objects would make a 'good shadow', meaning a dark, well-defined one. Amanda (P4) was so keen to make her shadow on the screen with a glass vase that any shadow she could make was regarded as a good one! This type of activity involved predicting, discussion as to the properties of the object and observation once the light was switched on. Richard (P1) even offered a hypothesis to explain his careful observation.

P1:   When you turn the light on the shadow is darker. It is different around the edges because light can get past a little bit.

The next activity was designed so that the group went away from the screen to draw on card a shape that would form an interesting shadow. We wanted to know if they would cut holes in the shapes to let light through. This session ended before they could test their shapes. Amanda (P4) and Stephanie (P5) were then interviewed and asked the same question, 'How is a shadow made?'.

T: Can you tell me everything you need to make a shadow?

P4:   Sun.

T: What does the sun do?

P4:   The shadow moves when you walk.

T: If the sun shines down on you do you get a shadow?

P4:   It's reflection.

T: What is reflection?
        (P4 makes no answer)
        How does the light make a black mark?

P4:   We must stand in the way.

T: What do we need to make shadows?

P5:   We need sun, flat ground and light. When people move you get the bit of dark.

T: How is the dark made?

P5:   The sun shines on your hand and can't get through.

Amanda's (P4) reply, 'We must stand in the way' and Stephanie's (P5), 'the sun shines on your hand and can't get through' is evidence of a developing understanding about the link between shadows and the blockage of light. By spending this session making and testing, looking and predicting the children appear to have become more confident in talking about and understanding shadows.

Session three, that afternoon, involved the group making shadows with their cut-out shapes. By now it was evident that they all understood that light had to be blocked to make a shadow. We wanted them to predict and test in a more structured way. We gave them a workcard with a silhouette drawn on it. They were challenged to make a shape that would make a shadow identical to that on the workcard. This involved predicting and testing and then possibly modifying the first attempt. The session worked well and the children were thinking carefully about the outcome of their work.

P1:   Can we colour them in?

T: If that will make the shadow better.

P2:   I've gone wrong.

T: Why?
P2:   The wheel should be over there!
P1:   I've done it (shows picture).
T: Does it make a shadow?
P1:   No. (cuts it out) I've done it.
T: Will it work? How will you find out?
P1:   Go and test it (Teacher tries to stop children leaping around and pupil puts her shape in front of the lamp).
T: Is it exactly the same? (Pupil compares the picture and the shadow).
        Can you change it?
T: Can you make the shadow bigger? (Pupil brings the template away from the screen).
T: It's gone fuzzy now. Did the colouring help?
P1:   No, it doesn't show up.

In our communication with the children we had discovered the starting point from which to base our study. We had discovered a few 'alternative frameworks' about shadows. We had encouraged the children to use process skills to see and experience for themselves the concept of light source – object – shadow. As teachers we had kept an open mind as to the scenario that was unfolding before us and reacted to the children, not the knowledge to be taught.

The teachers' commentary ends here.

Comments

It is clearly important not to make assumptions about children's existing understanding. The evidence provided by the children's early explorations in the playground were misleading and the first evidence of unanticipated ideas became apparent only when the children were asked to try to draw their ideas about how shadows were formed. The use of children's drawings and diagrams as a means of assessing their existing ideas is very valuable, particularly when supported by their explanations of what they have drawn. However, the real limitations in these children's existing ideas, and use of language, were exposed when they were asked to solve the problem of creating a shadow using a torch in the classroom. The confusion between a shadow and the intense pool of light formed by a torch was a crucial aspect of the children's understanding that needed addressing and would have gone undetected had the teacher not questioned the children appropriately and at the right time.

The alternative frameworks about shadows held by these children are similar to those identified by others (Piaget, 1929; Guesne, 1978 and Fehur and Rice, 1988). This research suggests children may hold numerous alternative ideas about shadows, including the following:

(a) A shadow has the presence of something with material characteristics;
(b) A shadow 'belongs' to an object;
(c) Shadows are alive and conscious;
(d) A shadow is formed when light 'reflects on', 'shines on' or 'hits' an object;
(e) A shadow is a reflection;
(f) Shadows continue to exist in the dark.

Adam (P3) provides clear evidence of a 'trigger' explanation, 'Yes, it hits me here [points to chest] and comes out behind'. Stephanie's drawing of a shadow with eyes suggests she may still hold on to the idea of her shadow being 'conscious'. The latter idea may well have resulted from experience of Peter Pan's shadow which always followed him or the occasional treatment of shadows as life-like, in cartoons.

The case-study we are discussing also serves to remind us that more than one experience is likely to be necessary to develop understanding of a concept. These children were provided with several experiences that were carefully planned by the teachers to develop their understanding. The initial unstructured activity led to much more pointed challenges and investigations that resulted in the children restructuring their ideas and appreciating more clearly that shadows are the effect of light being interrupted.

4. Restructuring in action

The following case-study features a boy, Peter, whose teacher has developed the desirable climate in which children's ideas are valued and in which there is freedom for activities to be either teacher or child-initiated. The case-study, produced by Rod Parker-Rees as part of the Assessment in Science Project

(Ollerenshaw et al., 1991), includes notes taken by him of children's utterances while he was observing a session that was some two or three weeks into a term. The term's work was focused on Big Ideas related to materials and their properties. The teacher's topic was 'School Buildings' – the school was undergoing some rebuilding and refurbishment at the time, including new chairs for the classroom. The earlier sessions on the science theme of 'materials' had included orientation when a large collection of building and construction materials was available for the children to handle. Following the elicitation stage the teacher had included a problem-solving activity: the children were asked to design and make a model chair suitable for classroom use. This task was completed, and, on the occasion of the reported session, it had been the teacher's intention to ask the children to design an investigation to test the stability of their model chairs. She knew that this would involve ideas of stress in relation to structure and the materials used, and of force and the need to measure weight.

This, however, was abandoned (for the two children Peter and Andrew) in favour of their own idea – to find out which chairs made the deepest scratches on the floor. The teacher felt this enquiry would be valuable, would still be within the broad area of materials and their properties and relevant to the interests and experiences of all the group. There followed the children's enquiry into a 'fair' test. Peter and Andrew discuss their ideas as they work. The utterances which follow track the development of Peter's thinking which starts with an explanation of events based on his understanding of the conservation of matter and moves towards a broadened explanation that takes account of the relationship between force, area and pressure.

CASE-STUDY: INVESTIGATING CHAIRS

Researcher's Notes

1 The feet on the chairs varied in shape and material (some
2 were plastic, some wood). After testing the chair with plastic
3 feet, loaded with Peter and a 6Kg weight (on unscratched
4 floor), etc. Andrew wants to sit on next chair. Asked if this
5 would be fair, Peter says 'No, 'cos I'm heavier than you ...
6 I'll sit on it again'. Finds 'a mark, but no scratch' (wooden

7   chair with metal caps). Andrew wonders if it would make
8   a difference if weights were on top of rather than under
9   Peter. Peter: 'It wouldn't make a difference because it's
10   the same weight – it's the same as turning a 1Kg weight
11   upside down – it still weighs the same'. 'If we spread
12   the weights out (on the chair) it would make a different
13   mark – no it wouldn't, would it? I was thinking it would
14   make a difference because the weights are spread out, but
15   the legs are still taking the same weight'. Andrew suggests
16   seeing what happens if they try with 1Kg less: 'No, you
17   couldn't – we haven't got accurate enough instruments'.
18   Asked if it would matter how weights were arranged on the
19   chair (preparing to test 3rd chair): 'No, it doesn't – yes, it
20   does! Because you're spreading the weight out'.

Clearly unsure, asked what he *really* thinks.

21   'No, I don't (think it matters) – it would be different but
22   only slightly because you're spreading weight to different
23   legs. If you put all the weight on one leg it would make a
24   deeper scratch'. 'My theory was right! The scratch from the
25   plastic chair is deepest. The weight must be spread about ...
26   more on these (wooden) feet because they're bigger. Or it
27   could have been the bumps on the ... (turns chair over to
28   show ends of legs). This has got more ... it's more rough
29   so it will make more scratches. Every bump will make a
30   scratch'. Asked if scratches would be worse if each leg had
31   a *small* piece of wood stuck to the end: 'No, because the
32   weight would fold the wood down so it wouldn't scratch'.
33   Asked which of   ,   and   would make the
34   worst scratch, Peter picked the middle one: '... because the
35   weight's going into one small area'.

Peter was subsequently interviewed by the researcher to probe
his understanding.

36   'I was saying ... the bigger the legs were, the more weight
37   it could hold ... it's spreading the weight, but if it had a
38   very thin leg it would make a deep mark because it's all going
39   into one area'. Could Peter suggest another example? 'If there
40   was a big building and it gets smaller down to the bottom
41   it's not going to be stable and it would put a lot of pressure
42   on one place and it would probably crack'. Could Peter

43   explain what he meant by 'accurate'? 'Something precise
44   to get the right answer – we couldn't measure how deep
45   the scratch is precisely'; an 'accurate' ruler 'has very small,
46   like millimetres and things and an inaccurate one has just
47   metres and centimetres'.

(Assessment in Primary Science, HPC 1990)

Peter's grasp of conservation of mass is secure (L 8-12) and he is obviously reluctant to abandon it even though previous experience of spreading weight out (L 10-16) and the evidence from their tests challenge his early statements. Gradually, as they undertake the tests (L 17-20), Peter is able to modify his explanation and draw upon evidence to expand on his ideas (L 21-30). His restructured ideas are checked in a brief interview where he is even able to offer another example of the same effect (L 39-42). The teacher had pursued the nature of scientific enquiry and retained in her mind a broad framework of 'Big Ideas' in science that allowed her to see and accept the value of the children's line of enquiry within an area of study.

The case-study also demonstrates, incidentally, avoidance of two monsters which lurk down constructivist pathways. The first is that it is not always easy for the teacher to keep in mind what the relevant Big Ideas are; one can get carried away on a tide of observation. This in turn means that the teacher, in the capacity of overviewer, may not perceive the most fruitful line of enquiry in time for intervention to be appropriate. The teacher in the case-study admitted difficulty in this area and pointed out that she found it of great assistance to have a careful choice of materials in use as these were a constant reminder of what the Big Ideas were. In addition she found that planning done with attention to detail and an eye on likely options also stayed in the mind. The second monster is that, as teachers, it is easy for us to become hooked on the efficacy of particular activities so that we become reluctant to change or abandon them. This is especially so if the activity seems a good one or if it is the only way we can think of for children to experience what we think they ought to experience. The reality is, of course, that the activities themselves are relatively unimportant. It is the ideas that are embedded in them that count. The fact is that children themselves are often the best inventors of activities that are relevant to their learning and are of interest to them.

5. Designing an investigation

Children's early attempts to move from exploring to designing an investigation, based on one of their own questions, require help from the teacher. The following case-study shows how one teacher provided this assistance.

Following a period of some two weeks of exploration activities on minibeasts a group of four Year 2 children began a discussion with their teacher to decide which of the questions they had raised previously would be testable. The teacher, Ann Orchard of Shield Road Primary School in Bristol, acted as consultant and guide as she went on to help them design their own investigation. This planning discussion lasted almost twenty minutes. The transcript, parts of which are summarised, appears with the authors' comments interspersed, marked by †.

CASE-STUDY: INVESTIGATING SNAILS
(An off-shoot of an exploration of 'Minibeasts')

P1, P2 etc. are pupils. T is the teacher.

The teacher sits at a table with the children. On the table are laid the sheets of paper on which the children have printed out their questions. The discussion begins:

T: Do you remember Emma's question? (pointing). Can you read it for us, Emma?

P1:   Does it take a snail longer to go across a rough surface than a slidy surface?

T: That was Emma's question.

P2:   I think it will go faster on a slidy surface.

T: What do the rest of you think?

P4:   I think it will go a *lot* faster on a slidy surface.

P1:   (Rubs her hand along the smooth surface of the table) Look! You see – your hand just goes along but if it was rough (demonstrates hand meeting resistance) your hand gets caught and it can't go forward.

T: You think that will be the same for the snail do you?

P1-4: (Agree)

P2:   If it was on the slope bit it would be even easier, (showing a sloping angle with his hand). The children continue to talk about the ease of a slidy surface for the snail's movement and a slope.

†Note that next the teacher reminds the children of different kinds of questions so that the decision-making procedure is clear to them.

T: Do you remember what we did? We asked which of these questions we could answer in different ways. Do you remember?

How does a spider eat?
Pierre **b**

Does it take a snail longer to go across a rough than a slidey surface? Emma **t**

Do animals prefer dry or damp weather? Mrs. O. **w.t.**

How long does it take a worm to grow? Dominic **b.w**

How long is a snail's birthday? Neil **b.**

Figure 4.1

Questions listed and categorised
b : books t : testing w : watching l : looking

Ps: Yes.
T: So some of them we could answer by looking at – and some of them ...
P4:   By watching.
P1:   And some by testing and some by books.
T: And this was one that we thought we could actually test; we could find out by testing. I wonder, now, if any of you have ideas about how we can do that? How can we actually test that? You're all quite sure it will go better on a slidy surface? (Pause). Just have a think for a second. (Longish pause). Have you all got an idea of how we could do it? (No-one answers)
T: Are there any other surfaces that it might be worth looking at?
      Between them the pupils suggest carpet, plastic, a piece of wood. P2 thinks the snail might get splinters. A short conversation follows.
P1:   Even if the wood was rough I don't think it will go in the snail. If you feel it (... touching the snail) it's quite tough and it won't go in. It's got to have a tough bottom to go along.
T: (To pupil 2) Anyway it's a kind thought. We wouldn't want to hurt the snails, would we?

†Next, the teacher introduces recording of brief notes early in their discussions:

T: (To pupil 3) Christine, would you like to jot down what we have thought about? Now what was the first thing we thought about?
P1, 4: A slidy surface.
T: So what was your slidy surface to be?
P2:   The table.
T: OK. Write it down, Christine, so we shall not forget. Now, what were the other things you suggested?
Ps: Chair, wood, carpet, metal, a book, a cushion.

†The teacher now checks their interpretation of 'slidy' and 'rough':

T: So we've got 'table', which is slidy. A carpet which is ...

P1, 3:   A rough ...

T: A rough one.
      You've got the cushion.

P2:   It's like the carpet.

P4:   The book ...

T: A book. What's a book, then?

P1:   It's slidy.

P4:   It's hard.

T: It's hard and slidy?

P2:   It's roughish.

It is decided to try paper and card instead of a book for slidy surfaces. The children comment that books have different covers. Glass is mentioned and glass with 'bumpy' patterns. Again a slope is suggested.

P2:   A chair is bumpy –
      The teacher reminds him that plastic had been mentioned and the chair is plastic. In the course of a series of random suggestions P2 mentions a radiator because it is bumpy.

T: Paul – do you remember what you thought of earlier – that we didn't have?

P4:   Yes – metal.

T: What is a radiator made from?

P2:   Metal.

†The teacher now reviews the list with P3 to keep the group on track:

T: Right – so you've got carpet, table, cushion, card, paper. Any others?

Ps: Chair is plastic and bumpy. Radiator, glass, a slope.

Two of the children are worried about the snail falling off a slope.

P2:   It can climb up glass! It won't fall off.

P1:   It's got things that help it. It's sort of sticky underneath and it clutches on. You can feel it clutching your hand (shows snail on hand). It sort of ripples when it walks.

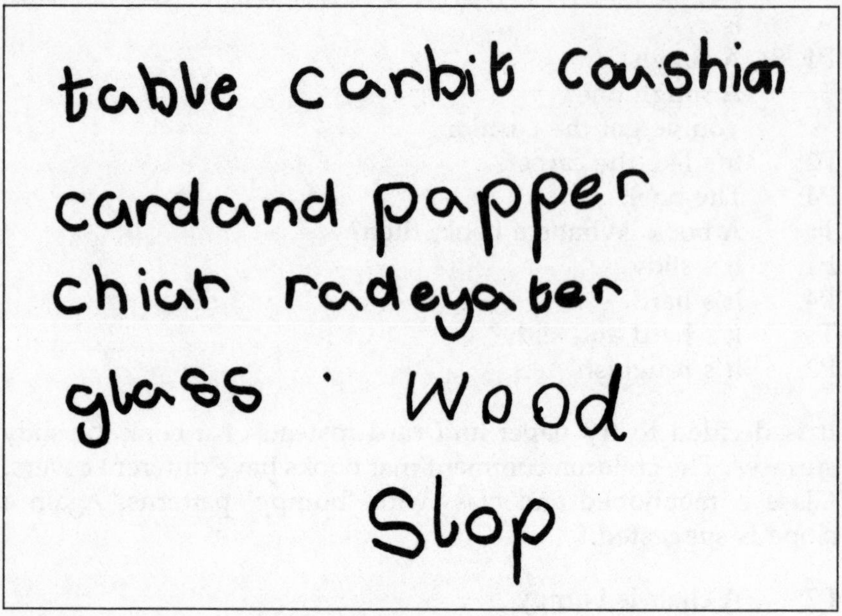

Figure 4.2   Child's recording during discussion

T: Well – we've got all these ideas and surfaces to try. Now,
        how are we going to do this? What are we going to do?
        Shall I write it down for you now? (Takes paper and pencil
        from P3).

†The teacher, here, guides them into the important decisions of
procedures:

Ps: Yes.
T: So, what are you going to do first?
P2:   Find the snails.
T: Right (writes it).
        Will we have a problem with that?

†The teacher is helping the children to be systematic in their
planning and to consider likely difficulties before they handicap
the investigating.

P3:   No, because we've got loads in the classroom.
T: What's next?
P4:   Find the things to go on.

P3:	To see if they are as good as each other (the surfaces). (Teacher writes this down).
P2:	By timing them (the snails).
P1:	Write it in your books (These entries are added).
T:	Are there any problems?
P2:	What if the snails keep falling down? That could be a problem.
P1:	If it's a grippy surface to climb up it will be all right.
T:	We put slopes in at the bottom of this list.
P1:	We can have: a flat slidy surface, a flat rough surface, a rough sloping surface, and a slidy sloping surface. (The child articulated this slowly but unhesitatingly).

†The teacher suggests a way of limiting investigation to make it manageable.

T:	I'm wondering whether we will have time to try all these today. Shall we just do the flat surfaces today? (short pause)
T:	So what are we going to do?
P2:	Find the snails.
P3:	Find the flat surfaces.
P1:	Time them.
P3:	... and write it in our books.
T:	How are we going to know how far they go?
P2:	Time them.

†The teacher helps the children to be explicit about their vague reference to timing:

T:	What are you going to time? Time them doing what?
P1:	How far they go.
P2:	Or if they go faster. Like on the slippy surface they go faster than on the grippy surface.
P3:	The rough surface
P1:	But if they decided to turn (indicating a curve with her arm) they would go further so we'd have to keep stopping the timer 'til they got back straight again.
T:	Is there any way of measuring how far it goes if it does turn?

†Possible problems with snail behaviour emerge:

P2:   A ruler?

T: Emma is saying if a snail turns (draws a large curve). You've measured curved distances before. How did you do it?

P3:   With multi-link.

†The teacher focuses their ideas once again on timing:

T: What are you going to time? Do you mean let them go as far as they want and time that, or, do you mean let them go for one minute or two minutes or what?

P2:   It doesn't matter ... we could time 'til they get to the end (of the cushion).

The children between them suggest that they measure out the cushion's length on the table using the cushion as a guide.

†The teacher returns to the problem of the curve:

T: What if it does go in a bend?

The children remember a puppet-making activity during which they measured curves with paper strips. They decide to solve the problem of the snails in the same way. They suggest that they make lines along which the snails can go – channels, tunnels. (This is an alternative to accepting a wandering snail with all the concomitant problems of measurement.) They decide they can draw lanes on the surfaces with chalk. They can keep the snails in the right place by nudging them back if they wander out of their channel. Having asked the children if they have everything they need to make a start, the teacher leaves them to get on with things.

†In this way the problems of the design of the investigation are overcome. With prompting from the teacher the children work out solutions to aspects of the design that, were they to be overlooked, could thwart efforts at testing at an early stage. Unless key factors are planned in advance and based on expectations there is little hope of an activity being much more than a haphazard exploration. These children need the teacher's help. At this stage they had have little experience in designing investigations. With practice, groups like this will look for design problems themselves. It is clear from their responses that the

children in this group are capable of solving design problems and that it is with the procedure of systematic checking that they need help. The children's difficulty about what they intend to measure is interesting – it is a common difficulty. Measurements and techniques learned in mathematics lessons are rarely applied in scientific investigations. Again, children need help to transfer skills from one curriculum area to another. The whole question of speed is, of course, difficult because it involves a relationship between time and distance as a basis for calculation. The children's solution avoids the calculation. The relationship is not part of their understanding. Their alternative provides an appropriate manner of measurement that is well within their experience yet which is sufficiently revealing for the level that the test requires; by timing a snail travelling the distance of a cushion they will be able to answer questions about whether it takes the snail a longer or shorter time to get across one surface than another with different characteristics. In the event they further modify their design.

†The children discuss the size of the paper and card needed for the testing. A4 is the largest available in their resources drawers. They decide to match the channels on the cushion, the table, the chair, the floor and the carpet to this size. Rulers are produced to draw up the lines for the channels down which the snails will travel. The teacher returns.

T: I wouldn't normally suggest drawing on the table and the carpet but we can get chalk off easily. How wide are your channels going to be?

The children draw on all the surfaces intended for the test.

T: Shall we look at our original plan? Where have we got to?
        (Reading the list)
        1. Find the snails.
        2. Prepare the surfaces.
        3. See if the sizes are the same as each other.
        4. Time them.
        5. Record in books.
        Topic books are the last but what do you need before you start?

P4:   Topic books to write it down.

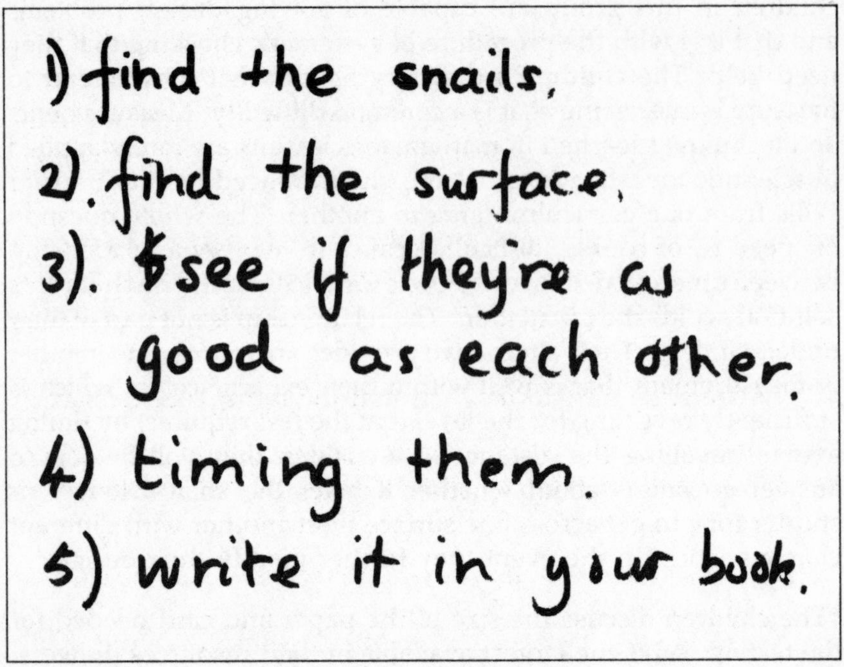

1) find the snails,

2). find the surface,

3). ǂsee if they're as good as each other.

4) timing them.

5) write it in your book.

Figure 4.3   Rough notes: planning procedures

The children get out their topic-work books.

T: Can you think of a sensible way to do it?
P2:   Big, middle sized and small.
P3:   Number of snails?
P2:   I was talking about snails – big, middle sized and little. Some might go slower because they are old and grizzly, like some old men!

One of the children suggests putting the information in columns. They all agree.

T: What will you put in the columns?

A discussion between the children to which they all contribute ends with the decision to have three columns:

Name of surface	Name of snail (Big, medium or tiny)	Time over the surface

T: Is there a quick way to enter which size of snail?

P2:   Yes, B, M or T.

T: Will you use the same snail for each try? Or different snails?

†The teacher's questions, here, cause the children to clarify exactly what they are about to do. The message is 'Think before you act'.

Between them the children agree that three snails will be used – one big, one medium-sized and one tiny. Each snail is to be tried across each surface. One of the children begins by placing a snail in a channel.

T: Christine has started – is that the right place to start?

The snail is a little way along the track. It had been placed behind the first line and, as a result of this, a rule about starting is introduced.

†Questions concerning fairness occur naturally. The teacher's interventions, both as directly transcribed and during the sum-marised episodes, prompt the children to resolve some of the considerations that might otherwise have pass unnoticed until after the event. It is difficult to achieve a balance in such interventions – the teacher might well see many more implicit unfairnesses than the children; to draw attention to them all will probably mean that the children lose interest. Here, the teacher selects the immediately relevant ones and those which are within the likely experience of the children. Other drawbacks to the design will be left to the children to identify after the event, if at all, when they review their investigatory procedures and their findings.

The children continue releasing snails, timing their crossings, nudging them back on line and then recording their results on the chart in their books. The movement of the children is a mixture of walking around, setting up an event, watching and timing, then sitting down to record.

It becomes clear that the boys are unsure about reading their stop-clock. The teacher spends a few minutes helping them with this basic skill. Sometimes children forget to write down the result of their timing straight away. The teacher reminds them to do it before they forget.

†All these procedures need practice. The teacher is enabling the children to identify the problems for themselves and then to find logical solutions. The 'don't forget' prompts are to help them develop good habits. The teaching of basic skills, such as using a stop-clock, is done most effectively at the time of need.

The watching, timing and recording activities continue for about forty-five minutes. As the children watch the snails they comment on what they notice: the slowness of a particular snail, the tendencies of some to stop, turn and 'look around', on movements that change their direction, on the trails of slime on different surfaces. A rule for the finishing line is established: 'The whole shell and body over the line but the tail can be on it'. The teacher brings the children together to review events. The snails are returned to their tanks and the children sit around the table with their charts in front of them. First they compare the results.

As the children read back the timings for each tested surface the teacher intervenes:

T: Which surface took the longest?
T: Over which surface did the snail travel the quickest?

†These questions might sound unnecessary. They aren't. Reading back results such as '14.05 seconds on the carpet and 6.42 seconds on paper, 8.31 seconds on the card', requires the children to equate the larger numbers with slowness and, in the case of closer results, to be able to do the necessary arithmetic. Handling numbers to explain activity requires practice.

Once they have discussed the charts and the results it becomes clear that the evidence is inconclusive.

T: Well, have you any thoughts about whether the snails go faster over rough or slidy surfaces?
P3:   Mine didn't like the slidy but he didn't like the carpet either.
P4:   You can't tell what they like best.
T: Can we say something about the rough and slidy surfaces or do you need to go on and find out more?
P1&2: We need to do more. We'd have to try some others.

Figure 4.4 Children's recording in columns

T: Were there any problems in carrying out your test that you hadn't thought of?
P1:   The snail kept moving round.
P2:   He kept looking up – I had to push its head down.
P4:   It kept going into its shell.
P3:   Sometimes they wouldn't keep on going.
T: Can you think of anything that might help to solve those problems?
P1:   We could dangle some food just in front of them and keep moving it away.

†This review of the effectiveness of the test has, for the moment, completed the cycle of events. The all-important opportunity to

compare results and draw conclusions from the evidence has taken place. It has enabled the children to recognise that the evidence is inconclusive. This reflection is followed by the teacher helping them to review the effectiveness of the procedures and the need to think of modifications to the design. Such thoughts and modifications may seem obvious and not worthy of the time it takes to probe for them. On the contrary, as is often the case in this work, verbalising thoughts helps to determine future responses. In this case the teacher is training the children to be methodical. The teacher now turns the discussion to what the children have learned about the snails and how they might explain what they have observed.

T: What have you found out about snails?
P4:   They're gooey and cold.
P2:   That's because they are slimy.
T: Why are they slimy?
P2:   So that they can stick to things and climb walls. When it stops it makes slime where it's been.
T: Where was the slime?
P3:   On the carpet – a lot.
T: Does it make slime all the time?
P3:   No it doesn't.
P2:   Yes it does but you can't always see it. If you hold a snail you can feel it on your skin.
T: (to P3) If it doesn't always leave slime why does it leave a lot on the carpet?
P3:   (Hesitates).
P1:   It might be because it's rough and so it scrapes off the slime so the snail has to make more.
P3:   It's a trail so it can go back.
P4:   There's no trail on the chair and the floor but it was on the carpet.
P1:   If it had legs it could go better and wouldn't leave slime. Why has is got one big foot? Why hasn't it got legs?

Answering her own question P1 continues.

P1:   Slime has something to do with having one big foot and holding the shell on.
P2:   If it doesn't have legs it needs slime to make sure it stays on.

T: What about the tentacles? (A child has previously
      called feelers 'tentacles'). Did you know about them
      before?

†This is a crucial discussion if the children are to extend their
knowledge of animals and living processes. During the conversation the children are invited to try to explain what they
had observed. (Explaining is a scientific function). This forces
them to think of reasons for the snail's 'slime' and the way
the snail moved. Their answers are logical interpretations and
closely linked with the experience. That there are other possible
answers does not make their reasoning wrong. To have considered
the snail's functions shows that they recognise that there *are*
functions that are linked with needs. 'Why hasn't it got legs?'
is a very significant question. It shows that P1 connects movement with locomotion and is beginning to consider the advantages
and disadvantages of different methods. A gate has clearly
opened for him; the revealed pathway may be intriguing enough
to tempt exploration, later.

Where next?

The children may well continue with modified tests that
allow for more conclusive evidence to answer their original
questions. What they wrote on the word processor
after this first investigation was as shown in, figure 4.5.
    Whilst this report is an account of the children's tests
and their results it does not, in itself, demonstrate the
important development of their understanding of snails. The
questions that arose during that final discussion may well
be pursued through reading: Why slime? Why one foot?
What connects the shell? What the children subsequently
learn from their book research will have greater meaning
for them because they have now formed reasoned ideas of
their own about snails from the direct experience of investigation.
    Encounter has become *useful experience* in two ways:
in learning the processes of investigative science and
in increasing understanding of animals. These two out-

> Our question was Does it take a snail
> longer to go across a rough than a
> shiny surface?
> we talked about it. and we made a
> chart in our books. We tested the
> snails and we timed them for the same
> distance, then we made a big chart.
> They didn't go on the table and only
> one went on the radiator.
> They didn't like the carpet at all.
> They liked the floor, the chair and
> the cushion and the card.
> They didn't like the slidey surface,
> but they didn't like the rough
> surface either.
> Emma, Christine, Ben, Paul.

Figure 4.5 Word-processed statement after test

comes work together and are interdependent – process and content.

The investigation and dealing with the independent variable

The children's investigation was 'to find out whether it takes a snail longer to go across a rough surface rather than a shiny (slidy) surface'. The independent variable was the nature of the surface. In this investigation it was either rough or shiny. This was a *categoric* independent variable. The decision had been taken about the variable and it was fixed. The child's original question 'Does it take a snail longer to go across a rough surface than a slidy surface?' was the determinant.

Had the original question been less specific the investigation could have been: To find out on which surface a snail moves quickest'.

The independent variable is again 'the nature of the surface'. But, this time, the surface could be anything depending on those tried. This is a *continuous* variable. It involves decisions about the number of different surfaces to be tried, together with the criteria and reasons for selecting them. Ideas of expectation have yet to be elicited and the problem redefined.

The first investigation is easier for children to deal with than the second. Even though there were decisions still to be taken, such as 'What is a slidy/rough surface?', the problem has been defined and based on the expectation that snails prefer slidy surfaces. The independent variable was therefore known and specific.

Children's questions

The foregoing case-study showed an investigation based on a question raised by the children. It also demonstrated how a teacher can help children to identify a question that is testable. Chapter 3 examined the strategy used by this same teacher to enable children to frame and categorise questions (pp. 61–2). We will now look at ways of making generalised questions into productive questions for investigations (Jelly, 1985). There are times when children do not raise questions from the exploratory stage or else they ask questions which seem unanswerable by any means. The reasons may have to do with the children's lack of experience in developed and probing observation (p.44). A first response to objects under scrutiny has a tendency to produce general questions that simply reveal the children's interest:

- How do snails' shells get their patterns?
- What are snails' shells made from?
- Why do snails have shells?

Answers to these questions are likely to have no meaning for many younger children since their understanding will probably be insufficient to make good use of the reply. A superficial grasp of theoretical ideas is less useful than the experience which comes from trying out ideas in practical contexts. It would be better if the teacher could pick up the interest shown by the children and convert such questions into researchable ones:

- Why do snails' shells have patterns?
- Are any other materials like snails' shells?
- How do snails make use of their shells?

Any of these three questions could be selected for investigation. The next step would involve breaking down the selected question into further questions that can be researched directly in activity:

- Why do snails' shells have patterns?
- Are the patterns on the snails' shells similar or different?
- Where are snails with similar patterns to be found?
- What is in the area in which you found the snails?

Once the children have collected information in response to these questions it may be helpful to prompt them into drawing conclusions about their findings:

- Could the area in which you found the snails have anything to do with their colour and pattern?
- Do you think the snails belong to a family?

Once children become accustomed to an approach of this kind they will begin to undertake the process with less prompting. Obviously the teacher's aim is to encourage the children to identify such questions for themselves.

6. Restructuring for children with learning difficulty

Some children may find it difficult to design investigations even with the teacher's guidance. Nevertheless it is still inappropriate to assume that brief illustrative activities will communicate desired concepts. Poor concentration does not necessarily translate into short activities. The following case-study resulted from the work of a teacher who was anxious to check his own ability to listen to and understand the children's reasoning well enough to help them link experience with new understanding. This case-study describes the work of a teacher, Mac Jeffrey, from St. Joseph's

Primary School in Bristol, with two ten-year-old boys with specific learning difficulties. The teacher was investigating whether he listened carefully to the children and responded appropriately. The work resulted from the spontaneous interest shown by the boys when some pictures were taken off their backing paper and they noticed the colour of the paper behind the pictures was darker than the rest of the paper. The teacher chose to tape-record the children's significant discussions for later analysis. The presence of another adult in the classroom on some occasions allowed intensive work with these two children. The teacher describes and summarizes as follows.

CASE-STUDY: INVESTIGATING FADING COLOURS

The children were given a piece of blue sugar paper, taken from a display board, which clearly showed a faded border. The children were asked,

- What has happened to the sugar paper?
- Why are there these different colours?

The activity was not directly linked to anything we were doing in the classroom so the children had no recent experience to draw on apart from their informal experiences.

As they started the activity I was immediately surprised by the level of curiosity and the investigational skills used by the children. I had anticipated that they might quickly decide that it was light, but that was not the case. They scratched the paper and then examined it with the microscope and magnifying glass. There was certainly more work going on now than was usually the case.

Their hypothesis, after many different suggestions, was that the air had affected the paper. I was very tempted, at this point, to influence the children. The Learning Through Science Project's Colour Pack includes a workcard on 'Fading and Fading Away' but it does not mention air and I had not considered it as an idea they might want to test! However, in this case, as I was concentrating on work with just two pupils, I was able to listen to the children and react appropriately. The children decided on a way to test their own idea by placing black card over a small area of differently coloured A4 sheets of sugar paper and arranging a display on the noticeboard. They were satisfied that the card stopped the action of the air over that small area.

After three weeks the children examined their display. There had been some slight change, particularly with the darker sugar papers, but nothing as significant as the example they had initially been shown. Fortunately the board they had used for their display happened to be in the shadiest corner of the room. Thank goodness! What if they had chosen the brightest area? They would certainly have concluded that their theory was correct.

After taking down their display the children examined the coloured sheets. The blue one again showed change but it was very slight.

T = Teacher; P = Pupil

T: What has made the change take place? ... What made the shading different?
P1: The air ... might be the atmosphere.
T: Why haven't the others changed?
P1: They are all light colours but these are dark. It is probably only dark colours that change.

(They look at the board in another part of the room and see there has been more significant change on sugar paper behind the displayed pictures.)

T: But that's a light one, not a dark colour. Do you think it could be anything else that changes the paper? Why have the display board ones changed, but yours haven't changed so much?
P1: They've been up longer than ours.

(The sun shines brightly on the display board)

T: Today is another good example of another reason why the paper might change. What is affecting the board at the moment?
P2: Sunlight!

The children found another display board to try out 'their' new theory.

Circumstances, plus a little luck, allowed me to react appropriately to what the children were saying and lead them into investigating another hypothesis to extend their existing understanding. Some weeks later they eventually reached the conclusion that light caused the sugar paper to fade, although Lee remained convinced the air had something to do with it. So there was plenty of opportunity for more experiments!!

Comments

This case-study again illustrates a teacher eliciting unanticipated ideas from children and allowing them to investigate their own hypothesis rather than his. This can often be very threatening for teachers who become overly concerned with the children getting 'the right answer' or who feel that they lack the scientific knowledge necessary to see the relationship between the children's ideas and a more acceptable scientific concept. The former concern was apparent to a certain extent in the relief the teacher obviously felt when the boys' investigation failed to give their anticipated result. In this case the outcome was certainly more to do with luck than appropriate intervention from the teacher. It does however, raise the very important issue of what role the teacher should have when pupils' investigations appear to confirm their alternative ideas and hypotheses. Ideally the teacher will be able to suggest a further investigation that will provide evidence to challenge the pupils' ideas. Alternatively it may be a good opportunity to introduce the value of secondary sources of information.

Secondary sources need not be restricted to written material. The use of television and videodisc material (such as Modular Investigations in Science and Technology – MIST) can be valuable when children need to experience phenomena that cannot be provided in the classroom. For example, some nine-year-olds were recently exploring their ideas about gravity and testing what happened when they dropped similarly sized objects of different weights. They tested what happened from waist height and could not agree which was hitting the ground first. It did not occur to them that they might hit at the same time. They repeated the test in the gym from the top of the wall bars, again without being able to agree on what was happening. The teacher then invited them to use a module from MIST Disk 2 which showed objects being dropped from the roof of a building. The slow motion facility allowed the pupils to observe exactly what happened as the objects reached the ground. Further discussion and 'thought experiments' with the teacher led to questions about what happens to things when they are dropped on the moon. Another module from the disk was then used which showed a hammer and feather being dropped by an astronaut on the moon. This was undoubtedly an experience they could not have had directly, but which proved, in the event, to be invaluable.

7. Explicit intervention to aid the restructuring process

Sometimes, during the course of practical work, the teacher will observe something that indicates a lack of understanding that needs tackling explicitly. In the following incident, two eight-year-old girls were trying to make a simple electric circuit. This is another example of restructuring during an exploration. The teacher involved was Maryon Holt, from St. Joseph's Primary School in Bristol.

CASE-STUDY: EXPLORING CIRCUITS

Claire and Helen had systematically tried out various ideas and had correctly set up the wires, battery and bulb. However, I noticed that one of the wires was snapped off at one end preventing the circuit being completed. I encouraged the girls to examine the wires they were using.

T: Go on with what you are doing, but see if it makes a difference which wire you use.

Helen sorted through the wires while I laid out the broken wire against wire with two bared ends. I invited them to examine the difference and decide whether or not this might affect what happened. The children decided it would and eventually arrived at a decision that the missing part was made of metal and that this was an essential factor in the connection. They then successfully tested their theory. I altered the next stage of the activity to include an investigation into which materials allowed electricity through. The material included all-plastic 'wires', bare wire and plastic covered wires to see whether it was the metal part of the wire which carried the electricity. All the children did this test to establish and identify how the wire worked within the circuit.

This simple incident, while indicating the importance of the teacher keeping a wary eye on what children are doing, also highlights the significance of the resources provided. Although, in this case, the teacher became aware of the difficulties the children were having as a result of the materials they were using it is very easy to be unaware. In particular, when young children are having early experiences with circuits it is tempting to provide them with plastic covered wires with plastic covered crocodile clips on the end. These are convenient to use and children can easily assemble successful circuits without recognising conductive material. The young child is unlikely to have had previous experience that ensures they know there is metal inside the plastic. It is far better to use wire with bared ends and without crocodile clips that might be more difficult to attach but which, at least, lessen the risk of misunderstanding.

The introduction of the unexpected into an investigation can provide another strategy for the teacher to extend the potential of an activity and broaden the possibilities for it developing children's knowledge and understanding. Scientific behaviour starts with curiosity and this can be fostered by providing children with surprises. A collection of woods being tested to see if they float or sink might include Lignum Litae (which sinks) or a collection of balls being tested for the best bouncer might include one which bounces in an unexpected way.

The teacher in the following case-study was providing a group with exploratory experience concerning the separation of colours in black ink, using chromatography. It was a large group of nine, six and seven-year-olds. It was one of her first attempts to observe children's response to activities systematically. The discussion was taped for later analysis. Each child, except Johnathan, had a piece of blotting paper with a dot of black ink on it. Johnathan had been given non-absorbent paper with a dot on it. Pots of water and magnifying lenses were available. The teacher was Jo Hoare who was at Southdown Infants' School in Bath at the time of this work.

CASE-STUDY: EXPLORING CHROMATOGRAPHY

They were asked,

- What happens if the paper is dipped in water?

Questions were posed during this investigation:

- How many colours can you see?
- What is happening to the shape of the dot?

The children's responses were varied and included the following words to describe their observations ... thin, small, massive, fireball, volcano, snake, punk-rocker, face, flower, waterfall, soggy, smudgy, fat, rainbow, sea, rocket, sinking, stripped-off, changing, purple, blue, dark blue, normal blue, turquoise, greeny-blue, red, yellow, brown, purply-brown, greenish, black, golds, light blue.

Johnathan's comments start with:

- Mine's still normal (as others begin to show a separation of the ink dot)

5 minutes from the start:

- Mine hasn't even changed colour or anything.

8 minutes:

- Mine isn't.

I then questioned the whole group, who had become curious, about why Johnathan's hadn't changed. They were all convinced it was because his had more water. I pointed out that another child had as much as Johnathan but suggested he try his in less water.

After no success Johnathan said:

- I think it's the paper, it's not soggy.

Lisa replied:

- It might be the wrong way,

to which Aaron (who appeared uninterested in anyone's sample but his own) added:

- It won't make any odds.

They turned the paper over and Jodie said:

- That's funny! It's not showing out the other side.

Lisa concluded:

- The paper's different

At this point the teacher encouraged them to look for differences and the following words were elicited:

Filter paper	*Non-absorbent paper*
wall-papery	smooth

hard	soft
wrinkly bits	flat
sticking up bits	

The similarities identified were size, thinness/fatness and colour.

Daniel still persisted:
- They should do the same as they look the same.

Johnathan wanted to try again:
- I'll put a dot on the filter paper and see.

Jodie was still thinking of other explanations:
- You (directed at me) might have used a smaller dot.

Johnathan persevered with trying filter paper and succeeded in getting the black dot to separate into a range of colours.

Later in the day they were asked to match the colours and shapes using art materials of their choice and the results were inspiring. Several children used a magnifying glass at this stage. Aaron was still thinking about possible extensions!

- I wonder what would happen if we put a dot of paint on some paper and put it in water?

The rest of the group jumped on this idea with their own suggestions of markers to try. They discovered felt tip pens were the most effective and tried lots. Johnathan was still observing and hypothesising:

- My green has gone into yellow and blue. If we put yellow and blue dots on the same paper we could make green if we put it in water.

The investigations were certainly underway!

Comments

Introducing the unexpected to develop understanding and to encourage an activity in a particular direction appears to have been successful in this instance. The novel aspect of this work produced an obstacle for the children that helped focus their observation and improved their motivation. This kind of device needs sensitive handling because it could equally well have led to frustration and loss of interest.

Children's existing ideas

It is evident from each of the case-studies that all children tackle science topics from the basis of existing ideas. These influence their responses and the way they interpret the language of the teacher and their peers. Recognition of the children's context for constructing ideas can help in interpreting the meaning. The theories of the world held by members of a local population are likely to have more commonalities than, and be different from, those held by a mixture of populations in different parts of the world, for the same reason. Toulmin (1972) refers to this as 'conceptual ecology'. Hewson and Hamlyn (1984) provide an example: the word 'hot' in a western context involves ideas of heat, energy flow and calorific value, whereas responses from the Sotho people of Southern Africa about the word 'hot' have implications of agitation, being disturbed and kinetic movement. Consequently concepts associated with energy will already have taken on slightly different meanings.

As Von Glasersfeld (1989) expresses it, 'Children, we must never forget, are not repositories for adult "knowledge" but are organisms that, like all of us, are constantly trying to make sense of, to understand, their experience'. Some differences between boys and girls in the way they handle materials and consider solutions to investigations is discussed in the case-study in Chapter 8 (p.204). Gender differences in experiences and attitude reflect the cultural variation of everyone's existence. Before children come to school they are learning higher-order cognitive and linguistic skills through the interactions of domestic life: 'Through these mundane interactions, children learn the accumulated wisdom and the cognitive and communicative tools of their culture'. Tharp and Gallimore (Light, Sheldon, and Woodhead 1991, p.42)

That the influences on learning are considerable is not in doubt; all we can do as teachers is be aware of what they may be and cultivate a flexible interpretative view of what we see and hear.

8. Summary

The idea that a single, logical, order for introducing concepts exists is not the experience of most teachers. None of the case-studies endorses such a linear view of learning. It therefore follows that if the teacher wishes to allow for alternative orderings of concept acquisition then due deference has to be paid to the children's intuitive ideas. If children are to understand new ideas they will need to develop investigative skills that will clarify and support their thinking in a way that is personal to them. When investigative skills become embedded in a child's working responses it will become unnecessary for the teacher to devise separate activities in which the skills are to be practised. It will also mean that the concepts involved will have a significance for the child that is linked with useful scientific concepts. Testing, for example, the stickiness of sticky tape for no reason other than learning to design a test, will became superfluous. The context of such testing-activities will be the focus of the investigation itself, linked to Big Ideas.

Avoiding fragmentary experience in aspects of knowledge and understanding is similarly important. The apparent need to cover ground at the expense of giving children time to build on their ideas is a potential hazard for the unwary teacher. During the Assessment in Primary Science project (1990) it was found that in the first term of the year's work teachers were helped to find out more about children's ideas but,

> this information was very seldom used to inform the planning of subsequent work. Often a whole series of activities had been planned in advance to tie in with a topic and there was not time to build on the ideas which arose from each. Confusion or partial understanding was left to be 'revisited' on the next turn of the curriculum spiral. Activities also often ran out of time before children had a chance to consider the significance of what they had found out; they would record their results but they often did not go on to reflect on what conclusions could be drawn from them (PIPE, 1991, p.13).

It was also clear that monitoring children's progress was more difficult in those situations:

> Unlike skills, which can be observed over a long period in the course of many different activities, opportunities to assess and develop particular areas of understanding may be few and far between. The order in which individual children come to understand different ideas will depend on their own interests and experiences and will seldom fit the order in which the Statements of Attainment are presented, (PIPE, 1991)

The clear movement from exploration to investigation based on the children's own questions and their identification of controlling factors will encourage an understanding of the part that 'reasoned expectation' plays in the systematic designing of an investigation. This will help to move children away from the notion that they are making accidental and surprising discoveries. J. Solomon (1980) argued that the problem for primary children was their tendency to wish to discover the irregular, the unpredictable and the surprising. This tendency is unlike the work of a scientist who looks for regularities, for ways to predict events and reduce the likelihood of the unexpected. This view of a scientist's work does not challenge the intention to be open-minded during enquiries or the importance of being persuaded by evidence.

Children's verbal explanations and recording during investigations not only help them in the construction of their knowledge but also provide continuing evidence of their learning. This evidence very usefully informs planning by the teacher and is also valuable as part of a record of a child's achievement.

CHAPTER 5

Children's Recording

Children's recording is their own communication of ideas and understanding using any medium that can be saved and stored. It is a very powerful support to learning and teaching. This chapter will include some of its different possibilities and examine explanatory rather than descriptive recording and its value to the child and the teacher.

Any form of recording can have many functions:

- It can help children to clarify their thinking.
- It can be used as a personal record by the child.
- It can be used as a vehicle for discussion between the teacher and child or between the child and other children or adults.
- It can be used by children to express ideas.
- It can be used by teachers to check children's understanding and monitor any changes in their ideas.
- It can be a source of evidence for teacher assessment.
- It can contribute to a profile or portfolio.

Since we are as much interested in what children think as in what they know we need tangible evidence of their ideas, even transient ones. Encouraging children to record requires that the teacher help them to see the appropriateness of their chosen form of recording.

There are three principal occasions when recording will have a part to play in science work and each is likely to have a slightly different audience and require certain kinds of recording:

(1) *As work gets under way*: first responses.
   Audience: basically the individual.
(2) *During exploration and investigation*: collecting data.

Audience: a working team that tries to agree a consensus view of events.
(3) *Following activities*: explaining ideas and communicating. Audience: the immediate working group and the wider community.

In order to show how different forms of children's recording suit the different occasions we will look at several examples taken from actual activities in schools. To preserve continuity each example is presented intact and the occasions to which the different methods of children's recording are suited are indicated as they occur.

Establishing early thoughts can include the writing of brief notes that identify particular perceptions or interests.

CASE-STUDY: EXPLORING MINIBEASTS

The Investigating Snails case-study, referred to in Chapter 4, began with the children thinking about and observing minibeasts. Some notes organised under headings helped them to observe with purpose. These were elicited during a brainstorm session as the topic on Minibeasts was introduced.

Occasion 1: Thoughts about habitats (for minibeasts).

When the children's exploration continued they collected brief data on the number of creatures to be found in each location, see figure 5.1.

Occasion 2: Looking for characteristics

See figure 5.2. Here is another selection of ideas from the same class.

Occasion 1:

** Ideas of the things we might need to know about each minibeast.
** legs
** face
** nose etc

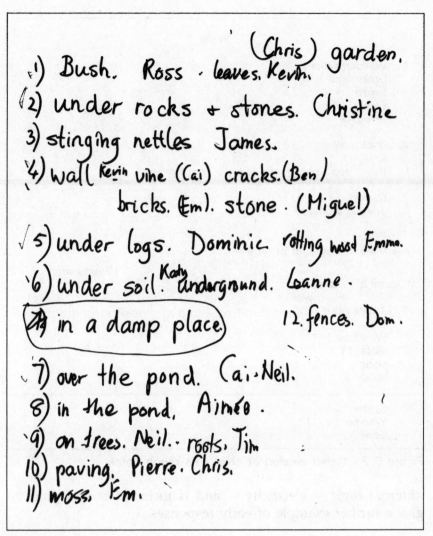

Figure 5.1

** This was kept available as a reminder

In following up these thoughts the children made simple charts to record their observations on snails, see figure 5.3.

Occasion 2: Looking for characteristics

Children's initial ideas may be the first entries in a floor-book. The following example (see figure 5.4), is related to a totally

120

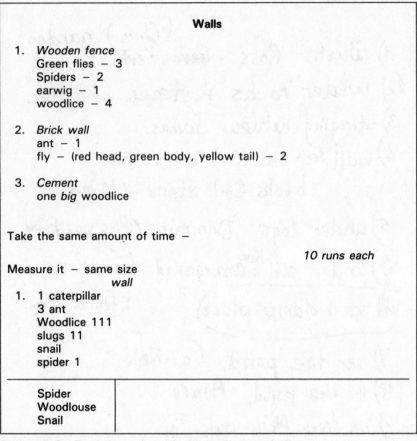

Figure 5.2 Typed version of children's rough notes

different topic – electricity – and is included at this point to give a further example of early responses.

Occasion 1. Electricity

Some year-six children had been asked to write three sentences about electricity. Their responses, (figure 5.4), which were recorded on the first two pages of the floor-book, had been written by them (rather than by the teacher – see Chapter 3).

These elicited ideas revealed the children's differing perspectives: Alex's vivid awareness of the power of electricity and Sarah's very practical recognition of the everyday need for electricity.

121

Joe   Snail   Pierre

legs   no legs
face   eye
eyes   on feelers
                    black

ears   non ears

Mouth   non Mouth

nose   on feelers

colours   black brown
                    yellow grey
                    green.

Wings   no Wings

out side   Shell
cold   its cold

smooth   Its smooth

slimy   Its slimy

Parts   no lines

squashy   noh squashy

Figure 5.3

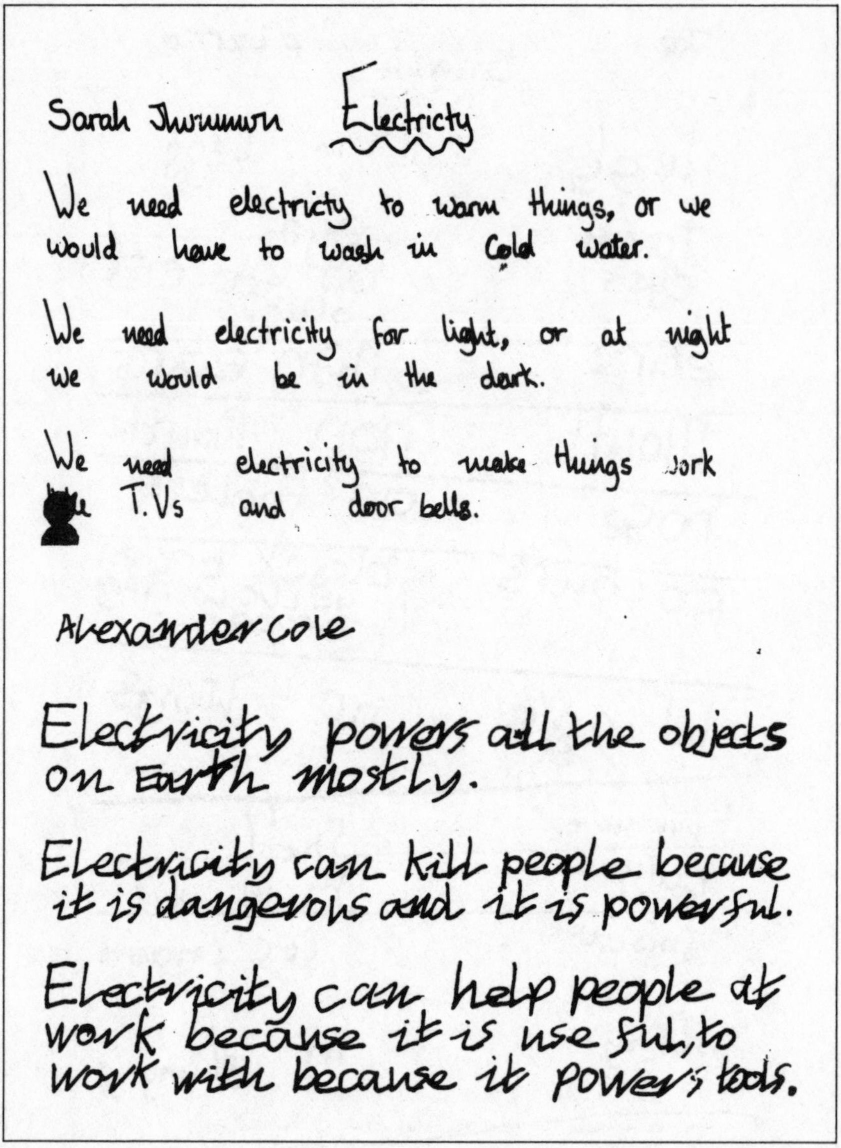

122

Figure 5.4

Following this the children connected bulbs into circuits and discussed what they thought was happening. They raised questions and undertook investigations. The next entries in their floor-book were illustrations of the children's investigations, see figure 5.5.

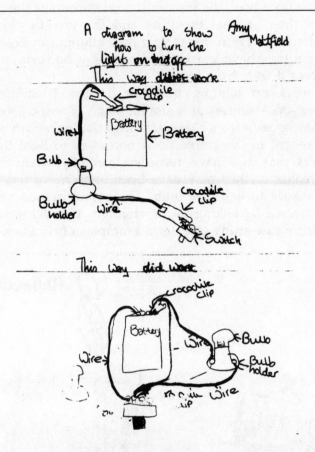

A diagram to show how to turn the light on and off — Amy Mattfield

This way didn't work

crocodile clip

Battery ← Battery

Wire

Bulb →

Bulb holder

Wire

crocodile clip ↙

→ Switch

This way did work

crocodile clip

Battery

Wire ← Bulb

Wire →

→ Bulb holder

main wire

clip

on

Using a Switch

I made the light go on and off by taking a battery some wires 2 crocodile clips a bulb holder a bulb and a switch then attached one end of one of the wires to the bulb holder and the other end to a crocodile clip then I did the same with another wire then with the last wire I attached one end to the battery and the other to the switch then I put one crocodile clip to the battery then the other to the switch then I move the switch and it turned on and off

Amy Mattfield

Figure 5.5   A record of an investigation (Occasion 3).

Later in a floor-book the teacher should encourage the children to review their original thoughts and the investigations they have undertaken. From this review the children can discuss and report what they have learned and comment on their change of perspectives if they have any.

Some work on lighting bulbs with Year 1 children produced floor-book entries at a similar stage of work, (see figure 5.6). It may be seen from these drawings that only Sam made an accurate record of the connections necessary to light the bulb. The others may not have recorded carefully what they did actually realise or they may have been unaware of the connections necessary to light the bulb. The correct reason will have been discovered by talking to the children. We will now return to the earlier case-study to extend examples of occasion 2.

Figure 5.6   Occasion 3. Recording an activity

Exploring Minibeasts

During exploration with minibeasts a range of recording methods was employed. Children made drawings of snails. They observed closely and used magnifiers to help. Some children wrote poems and created word pictures that revealed the detail of what they noticed and showed imaginative and cross-curricular responses to science activity, (see figure 5.7).

Sorting and classifying activities during the second week of exploration led the children to recognise and discuss similarities and differences between the minibeasts in their collection. The results of their discussions were recorded and clarified with the help of the data handling program, *Sorting Game*. This is referred to in Chapter 3 (p.61).

Ann Orchard, the teacher, reminded the children that they needed to choose two creatures from the collection to begin with and suggest questions that would distinguish one from the other. The questions had to be answered with a 'yes' or 'no', so an example might be 'Does it have six legs?' They were asked to suggest as many questions as they could before selecting the one they thought most appropriate and entering that, when prompted by the computer. They also wrote down their question

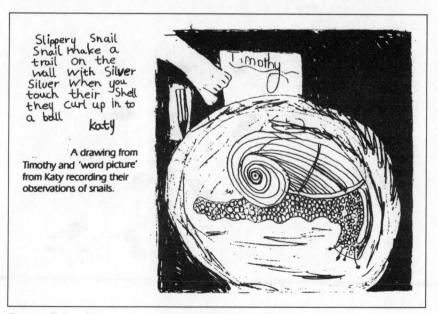

Slippery Snail
Snail make a
trail on the
wall with Silver
Silver when you
touch their shell
they curl up in to
a ball   Katy

A drawing from Timothy and 'word picture' from Katy recording their observations of snails.

Figure 5.7   Close observations (Occasion 2)

and built up a model of the key alongside the computer. They drew each minibeast to add to the end of each line of questions (see figure 5.8). The various parts of the key were attached with Blu-tack so that they could be repositioned if necessary when a new minibeast was added. The concrete building up of the key, although in some respects the most difficult part of the activity for the children, helped them understand the way in which the computer was organising the information they were entering.

The children used the program with a concept keyboard overlay (linked to 'Sorting Game' with the program 'Concept') that Ann had produced (figure 5.9). Normally these overlays are devised using the language the children have already been using as they talk about a specific collection (see MAPE, 1989, p. 15). However, on this occasion, the overlay had been developed through work with other children and was considered appropriate by Ann.

This activity, based on 'Sorting Game', involved children in formulating very specific questions based on their first-hand observations. Indeed, Ann required them to find questions that could be answered by others through observation. They were generally able to suggest suitable questions although it

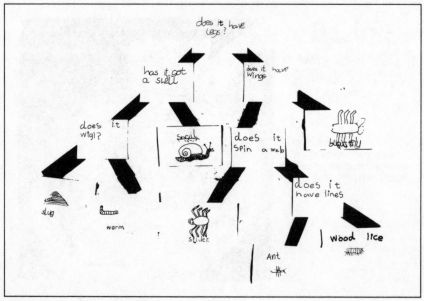

Figure 5.8 (Occasion 2)

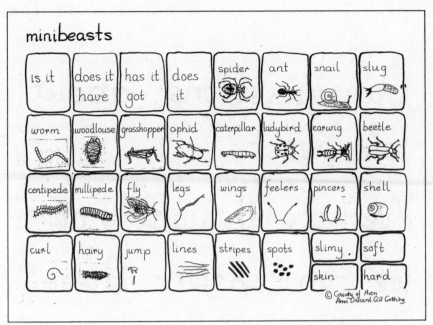

Figure 5.9 Figure A concept keyboard overlay (Ritchie, 1991b: 12-15)

How many legs does the
animals have?   l
Does it have a shell?   l
Aimee and Christine.

Does it slide ?/ Is it
smooth? t   Ross and
Miguel

          Were does the
slimy come from ?
Adam and Dominic   b

What does a non web spider
eat?   Emma w .   b

What does a snail eat? w.t
Does it have more than one
foot? l
Does it have a shell? l
And what colour shell? l
Does it jump? w
Is it hairy? l , t .
Does it have wings? l
Can it fly and does it
wiggle and does it curl up
? w
Is it coloured? l
Does it crawl? w
Shaney and Janine.

Figure 5.10

Our questions about minibeasts.

We have thought how we can answer these questions.

l - look.

w - watch

t - test.

b - book.

Figure 5.11

did become difficult for some, especially when considering a slug and a worm. For one pair, these two were eventually distinguished by 'Does it wiggle?' The groups for this work were self-selecting. Ann identified one child who was invited to choose one or two others with whom to work. She kept a record of who had worked on the program. During their time at the keyboard, and it often took 15-20 minutes for a group to complete a key, Ann was offering regular support and checking, by listing the questions entered, that the group was not having difficulties.

The resulting computer-based key was printed out for each group and then saved to disk for later additions or modifications. The key was also tested by other class members who, on occasion, provided constructive criticism about ambiguous or inappropriate questions, such as 'Is it big?'

The culmination of the exploratory phase can be identified by the questions raised by the children. The most convenient method of recording these at the time was the word-processor. The result is shown in figure 5.10.

The felt-tip letters at the end of questions shows the way that the children thought they might find some answers. The key to the letters was up on the classroom wall as a reminder, see figure 5.11.

This technique helps the teacher clarify with the children the differences between the questions. With the reminder in view the children may be encouraged to consider the nature of questions for themselves and the significance of testable questions. (See Chapter 4).

Occasion 2

When children are involved in field studies and collecting information about an area, noting where creatures go or how much they move about, it is useful to ask the children to compare notes and drawings. Doing this gives them a more complete picture. It may also prompt the noticing of curious behaviour and its patterns and, as a result, extend trial studies.

It is clear from the examples in this section and in earlier chapters that information technology can be useful in the recording and organising of children's ideas and findings. When children are struggling with complicated ideas Information Technology helps to free them from the distracting requirements of manual recording (writing can be practised at other times). Information Technology also produces a level of presentation that can reduce confusions and help children structure and restructure their thinking without having to interpret messy data.

Collecting data (occasion 2) demands that recording is systematic. Examples of this have been shown in the previous section. Data collected should have a purpose: to provide information that will help in the recognition of patterns, give rise to questions and provide evidence on which to base conclusions and further predictions. Early notes taken in the field, such as those on snails, may be transferred to a more visual record in graph form. Once again the computer can be a useful tool in helping the children to organise the information and produce it quickly and easily. The attention can be focused on the search for patterns rather than the drawing or colouring of graphs, see figure 5.12.

One group investigated the number of snails found in the same location on different days to test their hypothesis that there are more snails on rainy days. Decisions have to be made about the way the data will be collected and stored, whether in notes, or diaries, journals, grids, charts, matrices, graphs or pictograms. The detail of the data should match the level of the enquiry. For example, the children in the Snails case-study in Chapter 4 established a way of timing a snail which was within their understanding. The charts they designed to record the data (figure 4.4) were useful to them because they were straightforward and supplied enough information to help them draw conclusions.

The Snails case-study involved measurements. Measurement generally can be an area of difficulty for children. It is essential to use a calibration scale that is within their experience. If children fail to suggest ways of measuring that the teacher knows have been covered in mathematics sessions it is always a good idea to check their understanding of any system the teacher may go on to propose.

Notes taken during activities may sometimes seem unnecessary, particularly when something expected happens or where there is so ordinary an occurence that it holds no significance Such experiences often pass unnoticed or, at best, are trusted

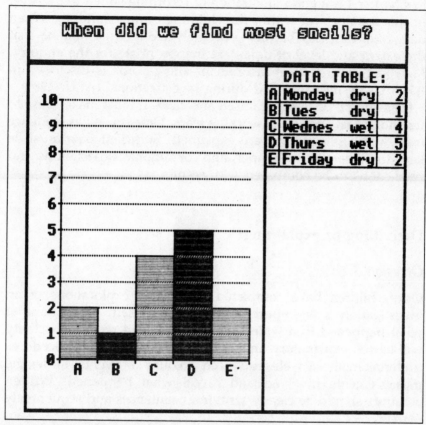

Figure 5.12   Snail survey results (Occasion 2)

to memory. Adults as well as children have been heard to say, whilst working on an investigation, 'Oh, I know what is happening here. This is no surprise!', 'I've seen that before', 'It's not going to make any difference'. It is as though the familiar means nothing and is discarded. Often nothing is recorded – and that is a mistake! The trouble with memory is that it deals in an impressionist and customised view of events. When enquirers feel that nothing useful has come from their seemingly every-day investigation it could well indicate their failure to have collected the kind of data upon which they could reflect.

Decisions about the amount and nature of data relate to the stage of an enquiry and the required level of sophistication. For example, the investigation phase of the Snails case-study in Chapter 4 is a good illustration of recording suited to the level of the enquiry and within the children's understanding. When data collection has become extremely tedious it could be that the extent and level of detail are inappropriate for the enquiry. Matching enquiry to measurement and records is discussed in APU 'Using measurement during investigations' (APU, 1989).

Data should be well organised and clear. It must make sense to the individual and to the working team. Data is used as evidence from which phenomena are explained. Sufficient data must be kept to allow this to happen and for original expectations and predictions to be compared with results.

Describing or explaining?

Occasion 3

Once children have completed a series of explorations or an investigation it is important that they present an account of what happened to a wider audience. A lucid record of activity will be self-explanatory and include a description of procedures undertaken, be a well-sequenced account of events, show the measurements involved and reveal what happened. Written accounts should be clearly written in sentences and sequentially correct.

Amy's diagram, figure 5.5, is an example of this kind of descriptive record. She demonstrates her awareness of the function of connections in a circuit that allow the switch and the light to work. There is a sequencing of her diagrams that helps an audience of peers and others to appreciate the steps that she took. She has organised her material logically even though her written passage is a little less accessible than her diagrams.

Another descriptive account, following his activity, was given by Peter from the utterance case-study quoted in Chapter 4 'Investigating chairs'. He, too, communicated his findings in a logical, economical and well ordered manner, as seen in figure 5.13. The main events of the investigation are briefly noted but show what they did and the results achieved.

Jenny is yet another child who offered a well organised descriptive account, this time in writing alone. It demonstrates

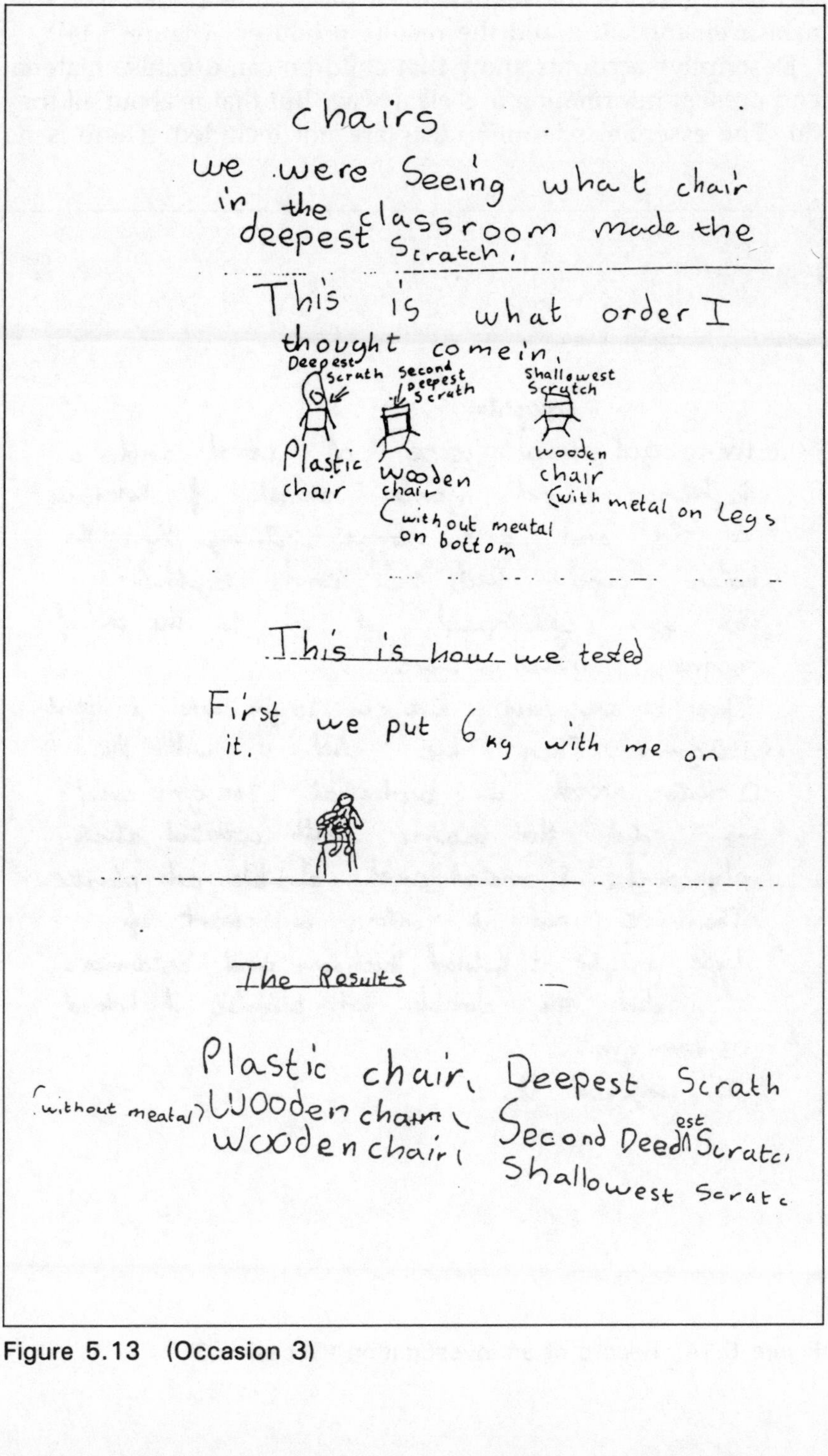

chairs

we were seeing what chair
in the classroom made the
deepest scratch.

This is what order I
thought come in.

Deepest   Second   Shallowest
scratch   Deepest   scratch
           scratch

Plastic   wooden   wooden
chair   chair   chair
           (without   (with metal on legs
           meatal
           on bottom

This is how we tested

First we put 6kg with me on
it.

The Results

Plastic chair,   Deepest scratch
(without meatal) wooden chair,   Second Deepest scratch
wooden chair,   Shallowest scratc

Figure 5.13   (Occasion 3)

her clear grasp of the sequences of procedures undertaken, the measurements used and the results produced, (figure 5.14).

Descriptive accounts show that children can organise material and present information in a clear way. But that is about all they do. The essential scientific ideas are not included. There is no

weights

we got a peice of wood and a tightener and made acople of holes in a tin and put some string throw the holes and tied the end together. the wea sellotaped it on to the end of some metal wire.
Then we went up in 10 gm and it bent at 110 gm. Then we did it with the Bollster wood it broke at 1200 gm and we did the same with cocktail stick, plywood, I metal and double arh plastic. Then I put it into a chart of type, weight it holded, thickness and estamate. I did the double arh plastic it holded 3 000 gm.
I enjoyed it.

Figure 5.14 Record of an investigation (Occasion 3)

explanation of why things happen as they do. Jenny did not offer any reasons for the difference in the results or say what she thought about the properties of paper, wood, metal and plastic and the way that properties might help to explain what happened. Amy did not tell us why the connections required to light the bulb with the help of a switch were necessary. She did not attempt to explain by suggesting, in her own terms, how electricity must travel.

Consider the case-study, 'Investigating Chairs', in Chapter 4 and what Peter actually said during the investigation. It is apparent that his illustration offers no clue of the quality of his thought or the depth of his restructured ideas. If all the evidence we had of Peter's activity was his written recording we would have a very incomplete picture of his understanding. Better use, therefore, must be made of children's recording opportunities in investigative science. This could involve only a modest change in what we ask children to do.

The following example in figure 5.15, 'Testing Lintels', is Andrew's summary report of an investigation. He has given explanation as well as description. We will analyse this in detail afterwards. This example of recording demonstrates more of Andrew's thinking than we learned of Jenny's, Amy's or Peter's in theirs. Andrew had been working within a group of eight-year-old children who were mixing materials together to find out which would make the strongest lintel.

In this example Andrew, who was testing the strength of lintels filled with different mixtures of sand, plaster and water measured in spoonfuls, has attempted to include information about what he thought would happen, what they did and what they measured. Finally, and significantly for the teacher and the reader, he included the reasons for his predictions and the unexpected result. He explained why in each case. We learn something of his thinking about the strength of materials containing air – in fact, his hypothesis. We might infer from his comment, 'reactat (sic) like a tube', that he has linked a previous experience of the strength of tubular structures with the current event. His idea is logical; he believes that tubes that contain air are strong structures and concludes that since the material (plaster-of-paris) is also full of air it is therefore strong in a similar way. Whether or not this is the connection Andrew intended should be established by asking him.

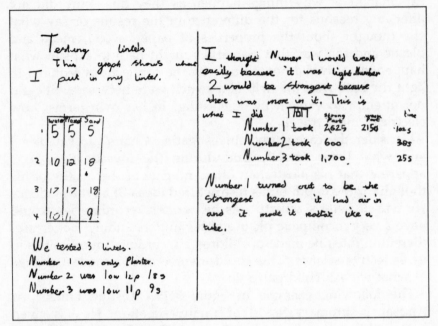

Figure 5.15 (Occasion 3)

When children are asked to give reasons for what they predict will happen or for what did happen it is likely that a hypothesis will be elicited, however disguised. For example, Andrew had begun by predicting that the second lintel would be the strongest. The reason he gave for this was, 'because there was more in it' (more stuff, a greater number of spoonfuls of the ingredients). This indicates that his hypothesis for strength is 'the more stuff the stronger the (lintel) structure will be'. Therefore Andrew had expected this belief to determine the result of the investigation and on that basis his prediction was made. However, Andrew's hypothesis to explain why he had predicted that the first lintel would break easily was, 'because it was light'. i.e. 'light things make weak structures'. This is not consistent with his hypothesis based on 'more stuff' for lintel two. It seems that he could handle only separate impressions of what were to be the important factors. The group had not selected either 'lightness' or the 'amount of stuff' to be what then guided the investigation. In fact what they had undertaken was more like exploration. They had not refined their questions sufficiently to plan a controlled investigation. Nevertheless a hypothesis was offered and as a result of the activity Andrew offered a restructured view of events, his new hypothesis being that structures with air in, like tubes, are strong – and, we must presume, even if they are light. His ideas obviously need clarifying and further restructuring. Andrew would be challenged to design an investigation of the strength of materials in relation to their weight or the confusion could be used as a starting point for a group activity on the same lines.

The point in all this is that even though Andrew's record of events threw up some apparent confusions in his ideas, it is valuable information for the teacher. Each aspect could be the basis of discussion with Andrew and the rest of the group. *Had the report on the activity contained only the measurements and the result, none of these points would have emerged.*

Of further interest are the discrepancies in his recording of the measurements. There is a mismatch between Andrew's 'graph' and what is actually written beneath it. For example, written underneath the chart is, 'Number one was only plaster'. The chart, on the other hand, indicates that the first lintel contained 5 spoonfuls of water, 5 of plaster and 5 of sand. Also, the chart lists the ingredients of a fourth lintel – a fourth lintel is not mentioned elsewhere. The information given in the written version 'Number 3 was 10w (spoons water), 11p (spoons plaster) and 9s (spoons sand) actually matches with number 4 in the chart. These inaccuracies may simply be the result of the hasty transfer of information from the on-going data collected during work in progress, onto the final summary report. On the other hand it might be an indication of muddled procedures during the investigation. Only reference to what the children said and did could help us to make that judgement.

Very young children can also be asked to explain why something is happening within their recording. It may be necessary for the teacher to act as scribe but all important connections for the child begin when they are pressed to think not only about what happens but also why it happens. Five-year-old Katie drew her account of some balloons being released. Her spoken explanation of why the balloons behaved as they did was recorded verbatim on the drawing by the teacher, see figure 5.16.

In her explanation to the teacher Katie has identified a causal link between blowing air into the balloons and the fact that when

138

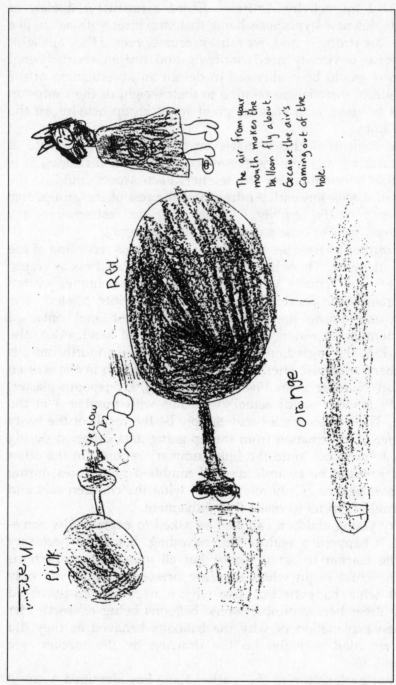

Figure 5.16

it comes out again the balloons fly about. In her illustration of the closely observed event she shows air coming out of the balloons, hints at their movement and indicates their different sizes and colours. This is a clear and accurate record made valuable by her explanation (Ref: also 'Jelly' drawing, Chapter 6). Whenever recording helps to develop or demonstrate the process of thinking it becomes valuable for child and teacher. Ways of helping children to make connections and then to explain what those connections are has been pursued with enthusiasm by many teachers. Another way that has been tried with children is that of concept mapping. This technique, used widely in later and higher education, has elements very valuable whatever the stage of development. It involves the identification of different kinds of relationships between ideas to develop an individualised picture of one person's understanding. Maps may be drawn at different stages in a programme of work and become a record, when compared, of the progression or changes in concept development that have taken place.

The example of a concept map shown as figure 5.17 was one drawn by a child, ten-year-old Sarah, after an event. The group of children had watched two candles burning, discussed what they had noticed and then begun creating their individual maps. The key words that arose during their discussion were the starting points for the concept maps. The word 'candle' was obviously pivotal and others identified included: 'Used up', 'Melts', 'Burns', 'Smoke', Flame', Solid', 'Liquid', 'Temperature'. These elicited words were arranged around the central idea of 'candle'. The children were then invited to draw connecting lines between any of the key words if they were able to write an explanation for the connection along the line.

As she has explained the links between the key ideas Sarah has been made to think about the relationship between various pieces of information about burning candles. She has had to move away from the simple repetition of learned information to think, instead, about the nature of each relationship. Complex inter-relationships can be explored through this activity in a way which would be impossible in linear reporting. Early attempts by children or adults tend to include remembered 'right answer' entries along lines when some bit of prior learning appears to be called for. As the connections that are made increase in number the distinctions between ideas become more refined.

140

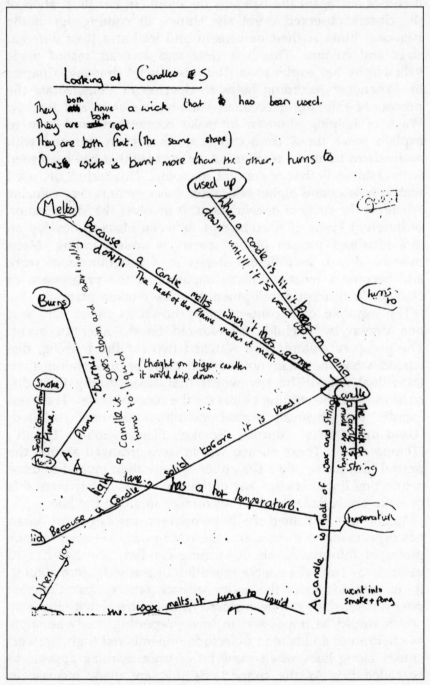

Figure 5.17 Looking at Candles

Broad connections are explained by the particular and specific. With practice, drawing maps helps to construct ever more individualised patterns of understanding.

Interpreting these maps helps the children and the teacher recognise the ways in which ideas are developing. Decisions about future work can be based on this information. The process of drawing a map also often reveals unusual relationships which might easily go unnoticed during ordinary thinking or in conversation. J. Novak and D. Gowin (1984) describe Concept Maps as visual road maps 'that show some of the pathways we may take to connect meanings of concepts'. The connections – the writings along the connecting lines – they describe as 'propositions' (1984, p.15). The authors describe concepts as 'embedded' in the connecting propositions. Partially developed propositional links or faulty links reveal, they suggest, varying degrees of concept understanding. This is why alternative sets of propositions cannot really be judged to be misconceptions. To the person who holds them they have a 'functional meaning' – they constitute current understanding which may need refining or developing or restructuring. The process of concept development is continuous. Concept mapping is a vehicle for negotiating meanings when it is undertaken with others. But it is important to say that although meanings are negotiable, learning is individual. An individual's concept map is an indication of that person's 'pathway' to understanding.

Concept mapping demands the expression of ideas about how things work. It teases out the connections between concepts. This activity needs practice. For children or adults who are more accustomed to recording a description of what they did or saw the shift to explaining ideas is quite difficult. Concept maps force the externalising of beliefs which often remain uncommunicated in the normal course of events. Making links can be encouraged by asking children to explain, in their recording, *why* something happened, as suggested earlier in this chapter. Simple mapping techniques can similarly be the forerunners of concept maps because, again, they challenge a child to think carefully and make connections between aspects of what they know. For example, some children who had been involved in exploratory activities on a collection of materials afterwards listed some of the materials and some of their uses. Then they mapped lines across to illustrate the links between them, (figure 5.18).

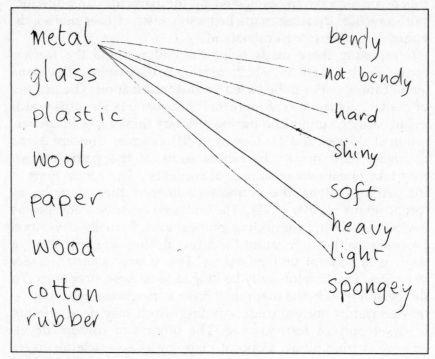

Figure 5.18

This activity took simple labelling, naming materials and uses, a step further. It pooled the knowledge of individual children to the benefit of all and helped to consolidate a habit of looking for links when new information is available. The next step in this recording activity was to list some of the properties of materials. These properties had also been mentioned during the exploration. The properties gave rise to a three column listing and drew out more complex relationships between the concepts associated with the words, see figure 5.19.

By using the children's own ideas this mapping procedure has helped to establish the purpose for examining materials in the first place and then, through the linking and clarifying of ideas, to create the basis of meaningful developmental work. Mapping has helped to make sense of an activity – labelling – which might otherwise have been seen as an end in itself and a sufficient record of events. This kind of activity can provide a useful lead into concept mapping in which ideas are challenged and conclusions redefined.

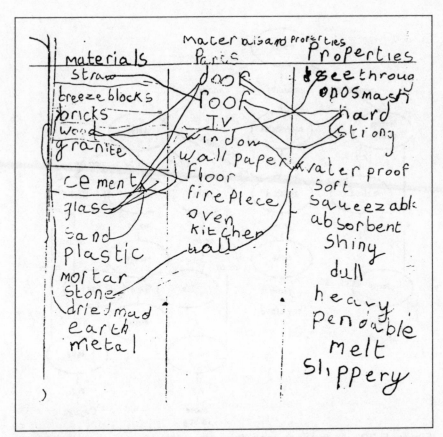

Figure 5.19

In their account of concept mapping J. Novak and D. Gowin (1984) discuss the need for second attempts at a concept map to allow for reflective modification so that a better representation of ideas can be produced. They also describe the value of arranging learned ideas into hierarchical structures in later attempts:

> Because meaningful learning proceeds most easily when new concepts or concept meanings are subsumed under broader, more inclusive concepts concept maps should be hierarchical ...' (1984, p.15)

This idea is illustrated by an example (figure 5.20) in which the more inclusive concepts are at the top of the map and the progressively more specific, less inclusive, concepts are arranged below them.

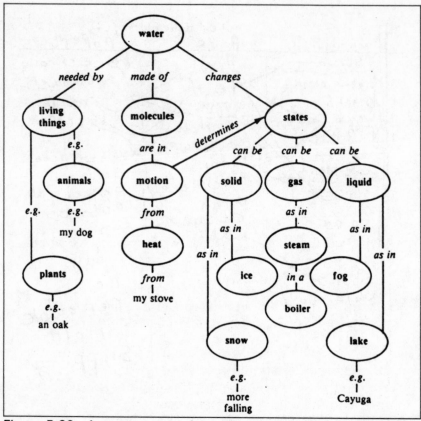

Figure 5.20   A concept map for water showing some related concepts and propositions. Some specific example of events and objects have been included (in Roman type outside ovals).
(Novak and Gowin, 1984)

It is pointed out, however, that the relationships within the hierarchy can change. What is being illustrated in a concept map at any one time is the networking in the brain that operates to support a perception of meaning. The meanings attributed to words constitute decoded experiences. That people may hold different ideas of the meanings of words as well as having a range of differing experiences to call upon emphasises the significant role of language in concept mapping.

Concept maps can support individuals as they try to make sense of experiences, help to make the intuitive explicit, clarify the connections between concepts that already exist in the writer's mind, stimulate the making of connections, be used to keep track of learning and aid the restructuring of ideas. The value of this strategy in cognitive development is cross curricular. Any discipline lends itself to plotting of this kind. It is an exciting way of developing alternative explanatory skills which will give learners a clear picture of what they understand. Maps are an example of a recording activity that can be undertaken at any time during the course of activities.

Summary

This chapter has provided some examples of different forms of recording and the varied functions they may serve. The three principal occasions, during science work, when recording has a specific part to play are:

(1) As work gets underway: first responses.
(2) During exploration and investigation: collecting data.
(3) Following activities: explaining ideas and communicating.

Obviously recording is also needed at times which do not constitute the beginning, middle or end of a process.

Recording plays an important part in aiding learning through sharing, and therefore negotiating, meaning. It will help to take an investigation forward by providing evidence from which conclusions can be drawn, and is most valuable, to the learner and the teacher, when it conveys explanations of why and how things happen rather than when it merely describes the happening.

CHAPTER 6

Assessment and Record-keeping

Introduction

Assessment is a process of collecting evidence of children's learning and making judgements about that evidence. Teachers' recording is about deciding what, of the evidence collected and the subsequent judgements, is significant enough to be retained and then implementing appropriate methods of storage and retrieval. In this chapter we will look at:

(1) The reasons for assessment
(2) The aspects to be assessed
(3) Recognising significance
(4) Dealing with the evidence
(5) Children's self-assessment and reviewing
(6) Reasons for recording
(7) The nature and content of records
(8) A framework for keeping records
(9) Liaison with parents
(10) Summary

1. *The reasons for assessment*

As we have already tried to make plain in this book, the simple answer to this question is that without assessing a child a teacher is not able to make appropriate decisions about the next stage of the child's learning. Chasing this thought to ground brings one face to face with the fact that the act of teaching has two main components – assessment and an actioned response. It follows from this that teaching without assessment is hardly teaching at all; it might be seen, rather, as a ritual derived, one might say, from the imagination of an adult, performed, often with their collusion, in the presence of children. In the 'Assessment in Primary Science' project (PIPE 1991, Ollerenshaw et al., 1991) the term 'constructive teacher assessment' was used to describe the crucial function of assessment to the teachers involved.

Reasons for assessment have been identified by various authorities (Cavendish et al., 1990; Harlen, 1992, p.159; Russell and Harlen, 1990, p.6) such as:

(1) Identifying children's progress through a scheme of work.
(2) Diagnosing a learner's specific difficulties.
(3) Collecting evidence to inform an evaluation of a programme of work, or of the performance of a class, a school or LEA.
(4) Satisfying national, LEA or school requirements and guidelines.
(5) Reporting to parents and others.
(6) Providing feedback to children about their learning.
(7) Ensuring continuity of experience throughout a child's schooling.

Of these, numbers 1,2,6,7 and, arguably, 3, are subdivisions of the core assessment function in teaching. 4 and 5 support the social context of education. In constructivist terms 4 and 5 are better described as applications of assessment, rather than reasons for it, however important these applications are.

It must also be said that none of the items on this list actually embraces the indivisibility of teaching and assessment. They do not challenge the commonly held view that, having been taught, children are assessed to find out, for various purposes, how much they have learned. It is this traditional view that has spawned much of the resentment to what, in these early days of the National Curriculum, are sometimes seen as assessment requirements 'additional to' the already burdensome demands of a teaching day. It is a pity. To the established constructivist the teaching day is naturally permeated with the implications of assessment: in direct exchanges with children, in short and long-term planning connected with learning, in organisation, in curriculum planning and in policy-making. All these are rooted in the continuous collection of evidence and the decisions that follow. The constructivist, abounding in direct evidence of children's learning, might well question the need for national testing but never the need for assessment. Assessment is not additional to teaching; it is central to it.

2. The aspects to be assessed

Science in schools has been discussed, in this book and elsewhere, in terms of

- skills;
- knowledge and understanding
- attitudes.

These three strands usefully categorise the field open to assessment. We will take one strand at a time, although, as we have constantly tried to emphasise, the strands are inextricably woven together in the experience of the learner.

Assessing skills in science

Science skills such as observing, predicting, hypothesising and fair-testing make up Attainment Target 1 of the Science National Curriculum and primary teachers are expected to ensure that fifty per cent of their assessments of children's learning in science is focused on these skills and processes. This requirement reflects a view of science education, widely held and explicit throughout this book, that through the appropriate use of scientific skills children come to a better understanding of ideas about the physical and natural world. As all children should now constantly use skills during their scientific work there will be numerous opportunities for teachers to assess the same skills in a variety of contexts. Each time children engage in a scientific activity there is potential for teachers to add to their existing picture of children's strengths and weaknesses in that area. Regular observations of children demonstrating specific skills will help the teacher come to a clearer understanding of how the same skills can be demonstrated in different ways. It will be evident, also, that children function at different levels in different settings and that the significance of a child's decision, for example, to check, measure or record, will depend on the context. Children working alongside the teacher, or peers, will demonstrate skills which may not be used when working independently.

Although any skill may crop up in any type of activity it is useful to focus upon the skills which are particularly relevant to the particular stage of the process. For example, our research in classrooms (Assessment in Primary Science Project, NPC, 1990) provided evidence that the following skills are most likely to be used in the stages of exploring, investigating and applying new learning:

1. **Exploration**
   Obtaining information   -   observing
   using secondary sources
   discussing

   Organising information   -   classifying
   discussing/reporting
   recording
   explaining
   finding patterns
   predicting/hypothesising

   Raising questions   -   predicting/hypothesising
   raising questions

2. **Investigations**
   Planning tests   -   discussing
   identifying and controlling variables
   estimating

   Carrying out tests   -   following written instructions
   controlling variables
   observing
   measuring
   recording/note-taking
   considering safety

   Reviewing results   -   identifying variables
   explaining/interpreting
   drawing conclusions
   discussing
   reporting
   recording
   hypothesising

3. **Application**

Recognising applications	-	drawing on relevant experience
		identifying needs and opportunities
Problem solving	-	generating a design
		planning and making
		evaluating

It is our view that all these skills can be practised and developed at any level; the Statements of Attainment can deceive – very young children do make predictions and can plan tests, and older children are not beyond improving their observation and sorting skills as we hope the evidence from our case-studies has shown. Children can also be helped to see each skill in the wider context of the whole process of finding and testing ideas. Any attempt to isolate specific skills can detract from a more holistic understanding of the nature of science. We should be wary of fragmenting children's learning in science into such arbitrary compartmentalised skills (see Russell and Harlen, 1990). The separation of skills, as a specific Attainment Target and in much of what is written about science education, can lead to teachers and children forgetting the inextricable links between scientific process and concepts. The constructivist model is firmly framed within a view of science in which the strands of process, knowledge and understanding, and attitudes, are inseparable in the experience of both children and scientists.

Opportunities for children to demonstrate their learning are dependent upon the teacher's role and response. Children often keep their hypotheses to themselves and, unless the teacher asks them to explain why they expect a particular outcome, will not articulate the basis for their idea. Perhaps the best way of helping children to develop their skills as well as to demonstrate them for assessment is to encourage them to review their own and other children's investigations: thinking about ways to improve them, commenting upon the clarity of recording, suggesting explanations for the results and raising questions to develop the enquiry further. The time taken by the exploratory and investigative phases of scientific work in the classroom often means that teachers regard the activity as 'finished' once the practical work is completed and the children have recorded the outcome or perhaps discussed it within their group. The benefits that can result from more structured reviewing are missed and opportunities to assess children's engagement in the processes of science lost.

Assessing knowledge and understanding in science

Unlike skills, which can be observed over a long period of time in the course of many different activities, opportunities to assess and develop particular ideas, or areas of understanding, may be few and far between. Harlen refers to these as 'infrequently occurring' (Harlen, 1992, p.168). The order in which children come to understand different ideas will depend on their own interests and experiences and will seldom fit the order in which Statements of Attainment are presented. The reorganisation of the Attainment Targets in 1992 to reduce the number to those related to knowledge and understanding does make the assessment requirements for science more workable. The adoption of three key ideas, (Big Ideas) related to living things, materials, and energy, means that children can be offered a range of different experiences, linked to one key idea, which will offer assessment opportunities for that content area. For example, children's understanding of the properties and function of different materials can be assessed during numerous classroom activities such as working with collections of fabrics, natural materials, building materials, balls or cooking ingredients.

There have been many strategies and suggestions for gaining insights into children's existing ideas discussed in this book. Chapter 3, which focused on elicitation, introduced one-to-one dialogue, group and class discussion, floor-books, think books, tape-recording, brain-storming, word-spurs, flow diagrams, posters and annotated diagrams, written accounts and concept-maps. All of these provide practical ways of collecting data that may be used as evidence, the last of them having particular potential for providing a picture of children's ideas. Chapter 5 considered children's recording and its potential in terms of assessment, in more detail. Each case-study has provided examples of evidence of children's knowledge and understanding which teachers have collected.

When planning activities and experiences for children it is possible to anticipate concepts that children may develop as a result of these experiences. Indeed, the selection of these concepts may well have been the basis of the planning. However, teachers should always be alert to the unexpected and not have their attention focused too narrowly; attention should not be limited by looking to assess specific Statements of Attainment alone. The Statements of Attainment can be used as guidance to help clarify ideas which might be assessed and the nature of particular levels. It is worth, however, reiterating the point that the Statements of Attainment in the National Curriculum are guidance and only the Attainment Targets are specified as statutory requirements. Further guidance for teachers in anticipating children's ideas can come from the growing literature concerning common alternative ideas held by primary children. In particular, the SPACE material can be a valuable source of this information which also provides strategies for appropriate interventions (SPACE, 1990-92). Knowing the sorts of ideas held by children in a specific area of science can inform teachers questioning and indicate particular ideas that need to be probed further.

It is unlikely that one experience or activity alone will provide adequate evidence for a teacher to assess children's learning in a specific concept area and further evidence will be needed, perhaps in a different context, to see whether the idea can be applied to a different situation. In terms of National Curriculum assessment, it is preferable to err on the side of caution and perhaps recognise the child as working *towards* a particular level, rather than too quickly deciding a child is working *at* that level. Regardless of whether the assessment is significant in National Curriculum terms, the insight gained from specific activities should provide information which will help in a formative sense.

Although the teacher will be exposed to evidence of every child's learning during a group or class activity it is often preferable to focus attention on a limited number of children during any one session. This way it becomes more practical to note and record significant utterances or actions. Strategies are needed to ensure this sampling does allow all children to be assessed over a period of time. Many teachers have also found it helpful to limit the key ideas they intend to assess whilst, of course, remaining alert to others where evidence presents itself readily. Holding in mind Statements of Attainment at *different levels* in the same strand of an Attainment Target is also desirable, since it helps the teacher avoid the temptation to 'assess the level' rather than the child. In other words, instead of isolating a particular Statement of Attainment and using it to assess whether there is evidence of the child being at that level, it is better to be aware of the statements within an Attainment Target strand at several levels and, having collected evidence of what the child understands, locate that understanding at the appropriate level. This is rarely straightforward. It can often help to discuss some of these judgements with colleagues and share evidence to clarify interpretations of the Statements of Attainment and how a child's understanding at a particular level can be identified.

Experience has also shown that children need longer to restructure and build upon their existing ideas than is often provided by teachers. This becomes even more problematic where teachers feel under great pressure to cover the extensive content of the science programmes of study. It is for this reason that the identification of 'Big Ideas' and the recognition that understanding in one area of science can be linked to understanding in another, can be helpful. The sequences indicated by Statements of Attainment are not the only routes to understanding; constructing concepts is not a linear affair, neither can the main ideas be hierarchically arranged.

Assessing attitudes in science

Can attitudes be assessed? The National Curriculum does not include Statements of Attainment for the attitudinal strand of science and the reasons for this can be traced to the original TGAT Report, which recognised the difficulties of criterion-referenced assessment of attitudes (TGAT, 1987). However, this does not mean that the fostering of positive attitudes like co-operation, perseverance and curiosity, should not be regarded as important aspects of primary education, nor that they cannot be assessed.

There are two aspects of attitudes that need consideration. These might be regarded as attitudes towards science and attitudes which are desirable when working scientifically. The latter are the attitudes which are most significant in terms of assessment and include:

154

- curiosity and the desire to find out (often indicated by the questions asked or the enthusiasm with which new experiences are approached);
- respect for evidence (reporting what actually happened);
- willingness to change ideas (in the light of evidence);
- perseverance (not giving up and trying other ways of tackling scientific problems);
- critical reflection (being self-evaluative and wanting to improve on ways of working);
- willingness to collaborate (encouraging others and welcoming the contributions of others);
- sensitivity to living things and the environment (handling animals with care);
- meticulousness (showing a desire to be accurate).

Evidence of these attitudes can be collected in the classroom in the same way as evidence of children's skills. Like skills, attitudes can be changed through experience and it would be wrong to think these are necessarily inborn qualities. Attitudes are often context-bound and children may well be curious in some contexts and apparently lacking in curiosity in others. Although the National Curriculum does not require teachers to assess children's scientific attitudes, if a learner's attitudes are to be improved then it is important that existing ones are assessed and decision about how changes might be fostered should be based on this evidence. Many of the attitudes listed above are, of course, generic and will be used, and can be assessed, in a variety of curriculum contexts.

3. Recognising significance

Evidence is what children do, what they say, and what they communicate in other ways – collected over a period of time. The two key points to remember are, in the first place, that a variety, a collection, of evidence tells a story. And a story is likely to give a more accurate impression of what is happening than a single statement. In the second place, while everything a child produces is evidence of something, the evidence we are looking for has to have some significance, a quality not always easy to recognise. Significance is a chameleon, with a habit of invisibility until caught in a certain light. The teacher also has to look for it amongst the daily output of a class of thirty children or more, which is a lot of material, especially since the quarry may lie in an utterance, a scrap of writing, a drawing, even an expression, a movement or a behaviour. It takes practice. It is not possible to store all physical evidence in the hope of perusing it during a quiet time – there will not be one long enough. All teachers can do is to keep some of it.

They will find they gradually get better at distinguishing between what children do while on the way to a realisation and what happens when they arrive. Every so often a child can be assessed more closely – a dialogue, a review of the folder, a closer observation in class, a recall of recent utterances – so that the changing position can be kept in focus. Doing this services the statutory assessment requirement. More importantly, it enables the teacher to become more sensitive to the holistic context of that particular child's learning. And that is the key to improving the ability to distinguish the more relevant evidence from the less. As the teacher's appreciation of a child's individuality grows so will the nature of important evidence become clearer. The skill refines. Eventually a half-heard utterance will emerge from a random background in a moment of revelation. Such instances of significance will become more numerous as the teacher becomes sensitive to the child's learning.

4. Dealing with the evidence

With developed assessment skills the teacher will begin to feel that moving in and out of children's minds is as natural a teaching action as moving around the classroom and equally essential. The teacher works in both locations.

Working with evidence at source

As far as the child-location is concerned, previous chapters have explained the constructivist model of learning and have attempted to relate teaching method to it in some detail. All that is needed here is to insert a reminder that the very act of teaching amounts to processing evidence. One or two implications of what has already been said are worth mentioning. To reprise: a child's current state of understanding has to be elicited. Information about it is carried in evidence. The process of elicitation is one of sifting what the child releases and of probing for what is retained. Judgements about validity have to be updated constantly and checks made when there is doubt. It is easy to be misled by language; children have been known to say the opposite of what they think. Statements often need reframing and representing before they can be acted upon. Similar dangers are risked during restructuring. Interactive group discussion at this stage can be misinterpreted. What, at first hearing, appears to be a child restructuring, or forming, a concept during the course of an exchange can simply be a child finding better language to express an idea that has not, actually, changed. Teacher-interventions at points like these involve processing of evidence in the same way that the formal exercise of collating and evaluating stored evidence does.

Valuing the unexpected

Processing, like hearing, tends to be conditioned by expectation. Statements of Attainment have the effect of directing a teacher's attention on pre-set learning goals. The expectation is, then, that progress will be defined by movement towards those goals. Evidence of movements in other directions can be filtered out unwittingly. In fact, some of the most interesting and valuable insights we can gain into children's learning result from the unexpected links they make between current and past experiences. Unanticipated evidence can be the most telling and teachers should be constantly alert to such utterances and behaviours. It is well worth noting them down as they occur; it is a time-consuming exercise but amply repays the effort in terms of helping plan the next step for individuals or groups. (See case-study 'Investigating Fading colours', Chapter 4).

Processing evidence in the classroom

Whilst collecting evidence the teacher is constantly making judgements: interpreting what meaning particular utterances and actions may have had; considering the influence of the social context in which the children are working; selecting significant evidence from the overwhelming amount of evidence available in the classroom; annotating examples of children's work to clarify what it indicates about their learning; deciding whether a child's written output needs to be complemented by further observations or questions; deciding which evidence to feed back to the child and how; selecting evidence to retain; looking for 'signposts' to achievements in other areas of science or other subject areas.

It is implicit in the above that assessment results from the normal work in the classroom. Assessment of this type is happening throughout the year; it is not something that happens at the end of a programme of work. Some teachers may, however, also set up specific practical or written tasks (or tests) to assess a child's achievements. These kinds of assessments were explored by teachers involved in the STAR project (Russell & Harlen, 1990; Shilling et al., 1990; Cavendish et al., 1990) and were used extensively by the APU (APU, 1983, 1984). They are the type of assessment tasks which now have to be administered at the end of each key stage. These specific assessment tasks, be they standardised, nationally prescribed, or school/teacher-constructed, all approach the assessment of science in a different way from that already described and the outcomes will be affected by the approach.

Planning from evidence

The constructivist's notion of assessment as a process should include the stage of planning a programme of work, since, as noted above, evidence of children's past learning should inform future plans. The demands of the National Curriculum mean that teachers have far less control over the content of programmes of work and they are required to plan within school and national guidelines. However, the needs of individual children should remain a fundamental consideration when planning. We consider this in more detail in the next chapter.

5. Children's self-assessment and reviewing

Children can be involved in assessing their own achievements in science from a very early age (Ritchie, 1991a; PIPE, 1991). There are ways in which teachers can facilitate this. Children need to be helped to develop the skills that will allow them to engage in self-assessment. The ethos of a classroom is also a significant factor in self-assessment. Unless children are learning in a secure and supportive environment where their ideas are valued and recognised it is unlikely that they will be prepared to be self-critical and reflective. Children need to be given the language to describe their own achievements. If their achievements in practical work are described by their teacher in general terms as 'good', the children will have little insight into their own use of scientific skills. Teachers who have tried to develop self-assessment skills in their children have come to appreciate how important it is to make criteria for success explicit. Children need to know exactly why their work is 'good'. These criteria may be the teacher's, or criteria that have been negotiated with the children individually, or as a group.

One-to-one dialogues between teacher and learner can be a positive way of encouraging self-assessment. A regular review time, when the teacher and child focus on past achievements and set targets for the future, even if it only lasts for four or five minutes, can have many benefits. The following case-study illustrates one junior teacher's development in reviewing with her Y6 class.

CASE-STUDY: REVIEWING IN SCIENCE

Jan Isaac, from Frampton Cotterell Primary School in Avon, met the idea of reviewing on an assessment course and decided to evaluate its use with her class of Y6 children. During discussion on the course the links between self-assessment and reviewing had been explored. She had used various proformas in the past for encouraging children to comment on their achievements in science but had been disappointed by their general and brief comments. She decided, therefore to use the proformas as the basis for the reviews she intended to organise. She selected several children to try out the strategy.

First attempts

The proforma initially used had three columns; the first was headed 'Activity' and was used to describe briefly the two or three science activities, recently undertaken, which were to be the focus of the review discussion. The next column was headed 'My comment' and was for the child to complete prior to the review. The last column was left for Jan to complete after the review. The children's comments prior to the review discussion remained general and often uncompleted. However, Jan found that focusing the children's attention on a past activity and helping them identify successful aspects of it, during the review discussion, caused them to revise and extend their original comments. One child, for example, had not completed his comment for an activity involving measuring forces and initially responded during the review with 'it was boring, I didn't learn anything'. After discussing the activity he added a written comment which was positive and identified his skills in using a Newton meter accurately. Jan's comments, written in the child's presence at the end of the discussion were positive and noted an achievement but also highlighted an aspect that could be improved.

A new concern arises

A worrying feature of the first round of reviews was the extent to which children identified neat writing and presentation as the criteria they thought Jan was using to gauge success. Even though she thought they were aware of the value she attached to practical skills and the way they did an investigation their perception was very different and perhaps reflected their experiences in other classes or the influence of narrow views of 'good' school-work expressed by their parents. In any event Jan felt sufficiently concerned to tackle the problem.

Exploring a new strategy

Her solution was to add another column to the sheet which was headed 'What my work will be assessed on'. For the next round of activities she approached the work differently. Before starting the activity with a group, or the class, she organised a discussion during which the criteria for success were made explicit. Some of the criteria were suggested by the children and she added others. Once these had been agreed they were added to the sheet. Sometimes, where the whole class was doing an activity, a photocopied sheet including the criteria was produced for each child. For example, a group was going to investigate the movement of shapes through different liquids such as water and wallpaper paste. The negotiated criteria were: 'a well-devised fair test; good collaborative work; using several shapes; shapes accurately made; presentation of results in an easy-to-read format; accurate timing; clear statement of what you found out.' This gave the children a clearer idea of what to comment about. Consequently, Jan found their comments more perceptive and useful, for example, 'Good test using 5 shapes. The times were nearly the same for the 3 tests of each shape. I got on well with Shane for a change'.

The discussion of criteria at the beginning of an activity had given the children some 'ownership' of the activity and its assessment. Their written comments provided a good basis for review discussions and Jan then set more explicit targets for each child, based on the review discussion. These reviews were part of the normal work of the classroom. The children were aware that they would get their turn and respected the time for other children to work with the teacher. The teacher obviously needed to organise the class in a manner that freed her to work with an individual for five or ten minutes. She was determined that the others should not waste their time on unproductive activities and therefore planned work for them which was self-sustaining but challenging. She also made sure that problems that arose could be dealt with without recourse to her. Monitors had specific responsibilities and if any pupils finished their task they knew what to do next.

The teacher had a clear purpose for the reviews. They were focused on particular science activities that the children had experienced. The children could prepare in advance for their review and remind themselves of the experience and their achievements. Analysis of a tape-recording of two early reviews helped Jan appreciate that her questions were leading the children too much to the 'teacher's answer'. She also found that she was using the reviews to teach and so decided to retain some information, in future, for revisiting in a teaching context at a later point.

Reviewing can be regarded as a cycle of four phases: recalling; analysing; evaluating and synthesising/target-setting (Greenway and Crowther, quoted in Mumby, 1989). The place of reviewing within profiling is discussed by one of us elsewhere (Ritchie, 1991a, p.31).

Self-assessment can have a variety of benefits (Muschamp et al., 1992; Broadfoot and Towler, 1992). It can help the teacher evaluate whether tasks are well-matched to a child's level. Children are likely to know better than their teachers whether they have tried hard (Fairbairn, 1988). Self-assessment can be motivating and improve the relationship between teacher and learner. It gives learners more responsibility for their learning. It helps to ensure that the purposes for an activity are explicit to the child, since the self-assessments made will indicate whether the teacher and learner recognise a common purpose. Sharing the responsibility for assessment with the child can reduce the burden of teachers without necessarily jeopardizing the validity of the assessments made. Children have proved to be more critical of their own achievements than their teachers. Self-Assessment can encourage the children to identify changes in their achievements by comparing present achievements with past ones. It reinforces the importance of competition with self rather than norm-referencing, where children or their teacher compare performance with that of the children's peers. Chapter 8 includes another case-study in which the teacher focuses upon self-assessment.

6. Reasons for recording

The central reason for teachers selecting and keeping evidence of a child's learning is that
- it enables informed decisions about the next and ensuing steps in the child's education to be made as they are required or when it is convenient.

The ancillary reason for keeping records is that
- it provides a store of information that will foster accurate judgements for other purposes.

Both these general reasons can be subdivided into specific reasons, in a manner similar to the reasons for assessment given at the beginning of the chapter. Not surprisingly, whereas the specific reasons for assessment were procedures and principles, being specific about the reasons for recording tends to generate a list of the mechanisms which support the procedures. This is quite useful. Thus, the central reason for recording, mentioned immediately above, divides into the specific reasons:

(1) To provide a focus for dialogue between teacher and child.
(2) To inform day-to-day planning.
(3) To assist the teacher's self-evaluation exercises.
(4) To inform longer-term planning for learning.
(5) To provide evidence for continuity planning.
(6) To service a whole-school review.
(7) To service moderation meetings between teachers.
(8) As displays, to provide a mechanism for sustaining motivation

... and the ancillary reason divides (in 1992, at least) into:

(9) To satisfy national requirements for evidence of learning in four Attainment Targets; the time and effort devoted to Scientific Investigation (A.T. 1) to equal that devoted to Knowledge and Understanding (A.T.s 2,3 and 4).
(10) To inform judgements of the levels achieved by individual children in all four Attainment Targets.
(11) To service the legal requirement for an annual summative report to parents and their right to a record of their children's achievements in each Attainment Target.
(12) To provide material for a summative report for a child's new school.
(13) To provide evidence to support a professional claim in a Standard Assessment Task (SAT) enquiry.

7. The nature and content of records

There is much variety in existing practice. Teachers in the past have tended to keep records of the notional achievements of children in this or that area of study. To that end considerable time and effort has been devoted to fashioning easy-to-complete pro-formas, usually tick sheets, often merely records of experience. Used alone, these present the problem that they record only the teacher's subjective judgements – which cannot be modified subsequently as the evidence which gave rise to them is missing. Samples of work were not nearly as frequently kept, except perhaps from practical or creative activities. The constructivist model of learning demands different thinking.

Also, in the past, much stress has been placed on the acquisition of isolated and simplistic examples of knowledge and performance. Tick-sheets can stand alone here. However, as enlightened teachers have always known, understanding is the key factor. For example, memorising the words 'Nam et ipsa scientia potestas est', can definitely be classed as acquiring knowledge. To be able to repeat them is positively a performance. The constructivist would smile at the irony of knowing the aphorism but not understanding the meaning, which is 'for knowledge too is itself power', (Francis Bacon). People who know the words but do not understand how they relate to English will, in fact, be powerless to use the phrase. They would gain the appropriate tick in the appointed box, though. So records need to include evidence of understanding and that is demonstrated in annotated samples of children's work or transcriptions of their utterances. These should be retained and considered to be 'records'.

Samples of evidence of work which demonstrate understanding will also show ownership of knowledge (but not necessarily, remember, the other way round). Similarly, of the comments which follow, those which speak of understanding will apply also to knowledge.

The nature of evidence for the record

Evidence kept 'for the record' can be almost anything, in any form. It can even be as minimal as a fragment of paper on which the teacher has had to add an interpretation of the child's marks – or supply a transcription of accompanying utterances. It does not have to be 'best work', if by that phrase is meant 'neatly presented work', although, in a negotiated selection of evidence for the record, children will probably need some persuasion that for this kind of record neatness does not always matter. Worthwhile evidence is anything that records the occurrence, and the nature, of a learning event.

Graphics

Many false assumptions are made about children's drawings and diagrams. These include:

- that the standard of drawing equates with the standard of observation or understanding which gave rise to it;
- that what is drawn represents all that was seen or understood;
- that errors in up/down/left/right relationships demonstrate lack of comprehension.

The dangers inherent in taking these bald statements at face value will be obvious to most teachers. It is easy to forget that different parts of the brain are involved in different functions and that, especially in young children, the integrating brain 'programs' may not yet have been written. It is enough, here, to advise that all graphic evidence should be subject to an explanation by the child and the drawing annotated before it is selected and stored, and we are confident that pursuance of this policy will produce many sobering surprises.

Evidence of understanding

Annotations can transform a piece of evidence. To show under-standing, or the lack of it, evidence has to demonstrate, or fail to demonstrate, the appreciation of a relationship in space or time, either in the form of connections between elements or objects or factors (space) or as part of a chain of cause and effect (time), or both. These are the 'explanatory' features described in Chapter 5. As we asserted a little earlier, children's drawings often do not reflect their understanding; equally their writing can lack the fluency required. In either case a teacher's note helps, provided it supplies the missing relationship or states clearly why the piece has been retained. Naturally, annotations should not be written until the teacher is satisfied the understanding really does exist and they should give the reason why that conclusion was drawn. In cases where probing elicits utterances which are evidence enough in themselves it is best simply to do verbatim reportage. In the following example a six-year-old had been engaged in a group investigation of dissolving. His drawing of what he'd observed could easily have been dismissed as showing little or no understanding of what had been taking place – until the teacher, in this case a researcher, asked him to explain the drawing. He wrote out the child's words onto the drawing as they were uttered. The result is shown as figure 6.1.

165

Figure 6.1

Apart from the startling discrepancy between the coherent thinking expressed in words and the undeveloped manual skills of the drawing, the two together show that the child has seen a relationship between heat and dissolved jelly, between cold and undissolved jelly, and has noted that jelly appears to dissolve in normal and soapy water equally. He has formed a hypothesis about where the (dissolved) jelly has gone and, with the 'STEAM' label, he gives a clue to his idea of the manner of its going. These last six lines (above), themselves amount to what would be an appropriate annotation of the child's work. Such a note should then be attached to the drawing and stored with it. Note that the writing of the child's utterances, though absolutely vital to the evidence, does not amount to annotation of the kind required. *Annotations are the teacher's explanation of what the evidence shows.*

In an HMI report (1990-91) reference is made to teacher assessment and recording pupils' attainments. It includes the following points which relate to the discussion in hand:

14. Many teachers retained samples of children's work so they had evidence to support their judgements. Samples of fairly recent work that were annotated to show where Statements of Attainment had been demonstrated provided the most useful part of a portfolio of evidence. Both children and their parents appreciated seeing the progress made by looking at carefully-selected samples of work retained over a period of time. Children sometimes helped to select work for these samples. This was worthwhile when the children had been taught how to make a sensible selection and understood about the qualities that their work was intended to demonstrate. (DES, 1992b)

Children who approach science work in the ways suggested in this book will have little difficulty recognising a 'sensible' selection.

Evidence of process skills

Evidence of process skills is far more often located in utterances, and in what children do, than in other forms simply because primary children tend to be more fluent in speech and action than in writing or drawing. Attention to speech as evidence repays the work that goes into it. One school, in Weston-Super-Mare, has devised a system for recording utterances.

A sheet is made out for each child and kept readily available (see figure 6.2). When a teacher is about to work with a group of children she clips the relevant sheets to a board and uses them to make note of any significant utterances, actions or significant children's recording. This is used across the curriculum. It is not adopted for science alone.

Another school, in Bristol, also adopted a similar system. This time there is also a note of future action. (see figure 6.3).

Communication problems

Where there is a language barrier between teacher and child we would like to think that speech would still be considered as evidence even if it involves the use of a tape-recorder and an interpreter. It would be impractical to make teacher-assessment and its related records, of children with little or no English, dependent on graphics alone. The teaching would be ineffective in many cases.

ST. MARK'S PRIMARY SCHOOL				
Name:				
Date	Assessment/Evidence	A T	Where	e

Figure 6.2

8. A framework for keeping records

The following framework is offered to clarify and summarise the range of different records a teacher needs to maintain in order to meet National Curriculum requirements and the other purposes outlined in section 6. It is a sequence of steps directed by the recognition that it is impossible for a teacher to retain all of the evidence of learning that is available in the classroom and that selection is required. It is also necessary to consider how children's achievements in science across the programmes of study can be summarised and used to meet the statutory requirements for reporting.

________ Primary School

OBSERVATION RECORD

NAME: Lee CLASS: 5C TEACHER: Ms. Bratt

Date	Comment	ATs	Future Action
4. 2. 92	Working with a collection of toys – group of 4. Understood a pull-back car had 'stored' energy before release.	>Sc4·2	
	Thinks 'acid' from a battery goes into a motor to make it work		Revisit during circuit work.
	Raised a testable question – Can a pull-back car go up hill? Do you need special tyres for different surfaces?	>Sc1·3a	
	Co-operated well with Robina		Use same pairing again.
7·2·92	Suggested speed of cars is related to weight (referred to knowledge of Formula 1 cars).	>1·5a	
	Measured with a tape (±.1cm) Had difficulties with stop-watch but persevered.	>1·3b	More practice.

Figure 6.3 (The child named, and the written comments, are fictitious)

Step 1 : Collecting Evidence

A teacher practised in identifying significant material will establish the base-line of relevance as the day progresses. This will mean that nothing of potential value is discarded until it is examined at Step 2. Transitory relevancies will be jotted down as teacher's notes. Children's recording, video and audio tape recordings, notes from review sessions with children, floor- books and notes from other adults working with the children, are all practicable forms of evidence.

Step 2 : Selecting and retaining evidence

This is the selection stage where collections of evidence are put together to form a child's record, which is then available for use by the child and teacher, as required. It can also be made available for parental inspection, for moderation and for other purposes. The means of storage will vary according to the nature of the evidence. A portfolio of children's work is an obvious strategy. However, because of the particular value in science of children's utterances and actions, Step 2 should also include some form of open-format record sheet which allows teachers to note comments about individual children, such as the examples provided in section 7. This memorandum allows a teacher to record any evidence which has provided an unexpected insight into an individual's learning or which provides evidence of the achievement of a particular target or goal. It is likely that such a record will be added to only occasionally, perhaps once a fortnight, but it will provide an ongoing record of a child's progress throughout the year.

Teachers use a variety of strategies to select a daily sample of children for such recording. Some do it very systematically; others add information only as it arises in the normal classroom context. It is essential that every child in the class has some evidence retained on a regular basis. Records of this kind, such as in the Burnbush example in figure 6.3 and Jenny Thyer's 'grocer's book' entry on page 189 (figure 7.4), do not always need to include as much detail as shown. Reference to floor-books or other sources of evidence may be appropriate and a system of referencing (including the day, date and year the work was produced), indexing and storage is needed. It is vital, also, to check that all evidence is annotated to explain relevance clearly. Step 2 is the stage of the recording process which informs future decisions and summative records.

Step 3 : Summarising evidence of achievements

The National Curriculum requires teachers to maintain records of children's achievements in each Attainment Target and a summary of some kind is needed to meet this requirement. This is Step 3 in the recording process. Such a summary, in science, should include sufficient detail to indicate achievement of particular levels within each of the four Attainment Targets. It could be even more comprehensive and break down the Attainment Targets into the strands described or even allow recording at the level of individual Statements of Attainment (SoA). The record could be a sheet, completed with simple ticks, but such ticks have limited value since interpretation is difficult. A more sophisticated means of completing a record need not be more time consuming and can be far more informative. For example, each box on a record can be completed in three ways; '/' means the child has had *some experience* in the area of the SoA(s), strand or level, and its related Programme of Study; 'X' means the child has demonstrated the skill or shown understanding with teacher's support, in a specific context and is working *towards the SoA(s)* or level; '■' means the child *has provided evidence* of using a skill, or understanding an idea, *independently or in new contexts*.

Although in some respects this level of recording has limited value in terms of formative assessment it can be useful in sharing with a parent, a new teacher or school, the child's achievements across the breadth of scientific experiences. It also provides *some evidence* for the teacher of coverage of the Programme of Study and areas of content that need visiting or revisiting. Evidence to support some of the decisions related to Attainment Targets will be contained on the open-format record or in portfolios of work. Other decisions about levels will have been made based on more transient evidence which is no longer available.

Step 4 : Producing summative reports

The final step is, again, a legal requirement and is concerned with producing an annual summative report for parents or a child's new school. These reports usually allow for limited narrative comment and, at the end of a Key Stage, are required to record the child's achievements as a 'level' for the subject. This single number, to represent achievement in science, is of limited value to children or their parents. However, in principle, there is no reason why a more comprehensive profile, maintained and retained within school, should not be used to report a child's National Curriculum achievements to parents since there is no requirement for the annual report to be a document given to the parents to retain.

The following example (figure 6.4) of an annual report for a child who is not at the end of a Key Stage comes from a primary school in Bristol (The child named, and the written comments, are fictitious). The end of a Key Stage report would, as mentioned, include additional information about the level achieved in subjects. Parents can request more detailed information about the level achieved in each Attainment Target if they give the school fifteen days notice.

The most effective way of maintaining these kinds of science records in primary schools is to develop them as elements of a whole-school approach to profiling or Records of Achievement (Ritchie, 1991a). Profiles are comprehensive records of individual children that cover a range of curricular and extra-curricular achievements to which children, their parents and their teacher, contribute. This ensures the children's scientific achievements are seen alongside, and in context of, other broader achievements.

9. Liaison with parents

In the context of learning the child, the teacher and the parent, form an important triumvirate. Primary teachers have always had regular discussions with parents about their children's achievements. The legal requirement for an annual report for parents is a minimum requirement and the established informal and formal contacts should continue in order to strengthen the partnership between home and school. The nature and quality

_____ PRIMARY SCHOOL ANNUAL REPORT

CHILD'S NAME: KATE REYNOLDS   Y 6   1992

ENGLISH	Kate has a very creative mind and has produced some interesting and imaginative work. Her handwriting is neatly formed and her spelling is good. She enjoys drama and handles discussion in a mature way. An excellent reader.
MATHEMATICS	She approaches new concepts without hesitation. Her investigational skills have shown marked improvement but she has the potential for applying herself more – this area of work. Excellent mental arithmetic.
SCIENCE	A highly competent scientist who enjoys practical work. She thinks through ideas and procedures well. She can generate complex ideas from the discussion of others but sometimes has difficulty in describing and clarifying what she wants to say. Her written observations + explanations are very good.
HUMANITIES	Throughout our topic work this year Kate has produced good results. Occasionally a piece is rushed but she has shown interest in all aspects, particularly historical themes.
TECHNOLOGY	Enjoys designing + making artefacts. She evaluates her own + the outcomes of others critically. She has sound keyboard skills + has mastered a simple word-processor.
ART/MUSIC	She has produced some excellent artwork + always participates enthusiastically in music-making. She is a competent performer, especially in the recorder group.
P.E.	Kate plays a full part in all sports activities. She is an able dancer + a reliable 'five' football + rounders player.

GENERAL COMMENTS

I have thoroughly enjoyed teaching Kate this year. Her confidence has increased and this has been reflected in the quality of her work. She is creative + able, and has started to realise her full potential. Well done Kate! She deserves + should do well at her secondary school.

Her best year of all!

CLASSTEACHER: K. W. Arnold   HEADTEACHER: Jane Somers

DATE RECEIVED: 17.7.92   PARENT/GUARDIAN: G Reynolds.

Figure 6.4 All entries are fictitious

of the discussions that are involved can be influenced by the record-keeping system that is developed by a teacher. It is our premise, and our experience as parents and teachers, that it is far more productive to start parental consultations (and reviews with children) with reference to specific episodes of learning, such as Lee's achievements whilst working with a collection of toy cars (see figure 6.3), as opposed to reporting general progress in subjects or even Attainment Target levels. Discussion of specific classroom activities can help parents put more general comments and 'levels' into perspective and context. Annotated examples of children's work from their portfolio, notes from a review session with a child, or a group's floor-book, can be particularly useful in presenting to parents their child's progress in a graphic and understandable form.

10. Summary

For the constructivist teacher, assessing and recording children's achievements in science is a natural and essential aspect of teaching. Decisions that are constantly being taken in the constructivist's classroom about the next steps required to meet the individual needs of learners must be based upon evidence of the learner's existing understanding and capabilities. The collection of such evidence requires teachers to be sensitive and alert to the actions, utterances and attitudes of children. It demands a range of skills such as active listening, focused observation, responsive questioning and initial evaluation of the outcomes of children's work. The development of these skills was the focus of the Assessment in Science Project, an outcome of which provided an INSET strategy to facilitate this aspect of professional development (Ollerenshaw et al., 1991).

Before ending this section on assessment and the requirements of the National Curriculum there is another positive aspect of recent developments that deserves noting. The need for teachers to come to a common understanding about assessments, and what they mean when they say a child is at a particular level, has led to regular moderation meetings and agreement trialling. As a result of these meetings many teachers have come to appreciate the benefits of professional discussions about the nature of children's achievements in science based on specific evidence of those achievements rather than upon impressions and beliefs which often distort professional discussions about education. Teachers, especially those teaching Year 2, have developed the confidence to be open with colleagues from their own school and beyond about the work they are doing and the outcomes their children are producing. This collaborative dimension of moderation is a theme picked up in Chapter 8 where we consider different aspects of teachers' professional development.

CHAPTER 7

Planning

The structure of planning should ensure that each aspect of progression, learning goals and achieved learning, is used to inform the others. This means that as children's learning is identified so the plan of work is modified and adapted. The advantage of this is that as the plan of work is better tailored to the child so the child's learning opportunities are enhanced. This is true of whole school planning as well as that of the individual teacher and is central to planning for effective teaching. A 1992 HMI report on Key Stage 1 assessment described some teachers as resenting the time taken to assess and record children's progress and adds that these teachers, 'had yet to appreciate the value of the information in matching teaching and learning to children's needs.' (DES, 1992b: 17)

Policy statements

For decisions about planning to have coherence they must reflect a philosophical framework agreed between LEA, governors, headteachers and teachers. School policies reflect a school's educational philosophy and represent a view of:

- curriculum areas and their organisation;
- ways in which skills and attitudes are fostered;
- ways in which concepts are developed;
- differentiated learning and equality of access to the curriculum;
- ways in which children's progress may be monitored.

It is likely that schools will have drawn up policy statements for each subject area and the main issues listed above. Policies will be consulted when a school develops its schemes of work. The established philosophies will be interpreted by and through a scheme of work.

Schemes of work

Schemes of work, based on policy statements, provide a detailed account of intended practice and the way children's curriculum entitlements are to be met. They are working documents that should be produced through the collaboration of the whole school staff. A scheme of work could take a year or longer to produce. A document, once completed, could then be used and reviewed on an agreed cycle of perhaps two years.

Whilst many primary schools integrate learning experiences for children it will probably be necessary to write schemes of work based on subject areas. This will make building the scheme of work around the programmes of study in the National Curriculum easier. Guidance about teaching approaches and methods of integration is therefore needed. When topics are used as a device for integrating much of the work in subject areas, the ways they meet the demands of the National Curriculum should be shown. Coherence in learning and teaching requires an agreed approach to the development of cross-curricular skills and processes, cognitive and communication skills, planning and social skills, to be built into planning.

The map shown as figure 7.1 offers an illustration of the links between policies, schemes of work and curriculum issues.

The document that a school produces will be specific to it. Getting a mix that works depends on the emphasis required by a staff and the children at a particular time. The examples that follow give an indication of different solutions to the same challenge. Each reflects the needs and understandings of the staffs involved.

Maggie Cosgrove, of Henleaze Junior School in Bristol, spent eighteen months, with the help of staff, piecing together a scheme of work for science. The curriculum at the school is taught by a mixture of topic and subject-based activities. Their aim for the scheme of work was that it should develop strands in Attainment Targets 2, 3 and 4 by using the skills in Attainment Target 1. The staff working group met for brief lunchtime and holiday meetings.

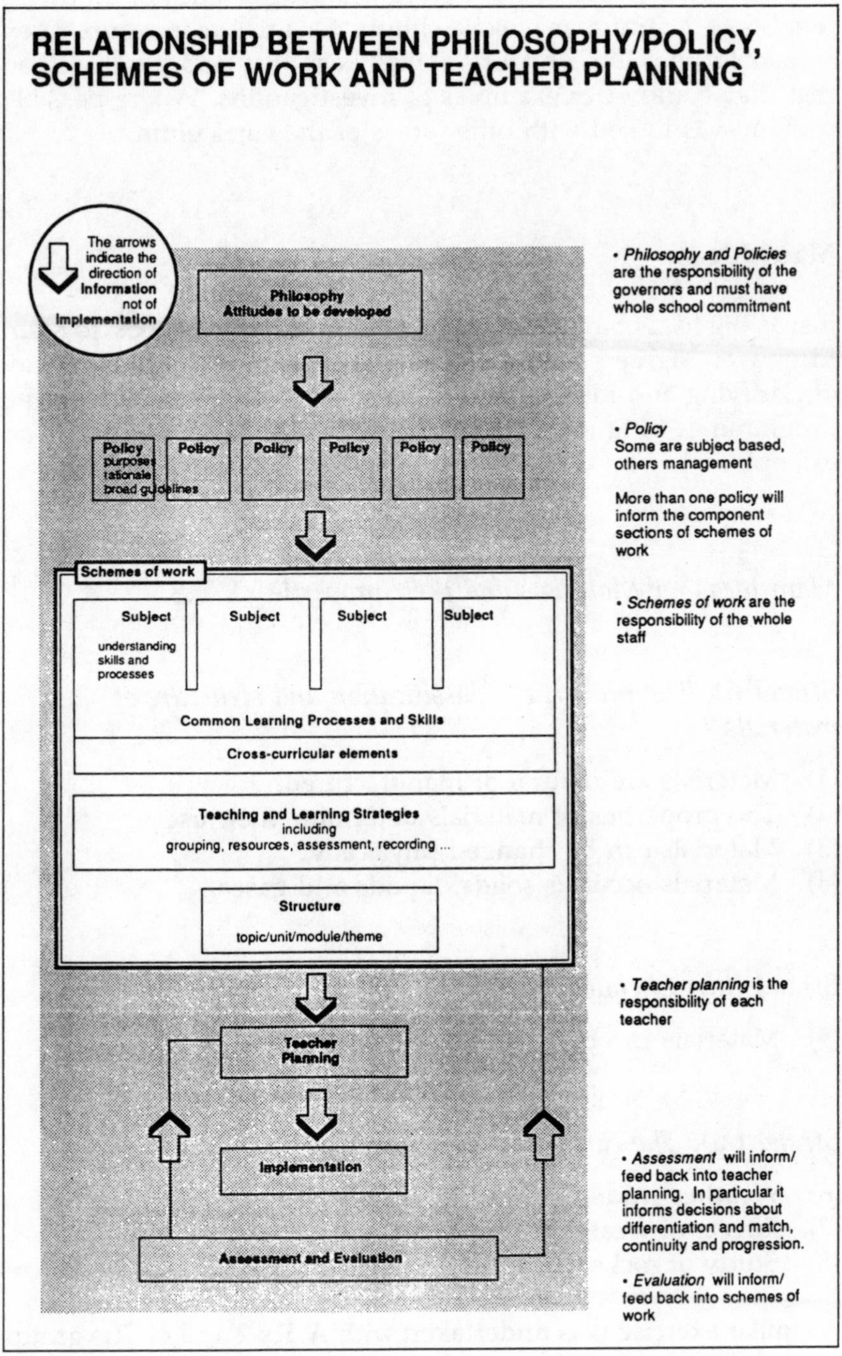
RELATIONSHIP BETWEEN PHILOSOPHY/POLICY, SCHEMES OF WORK AND TEACHER PLANNING
The arrows indicate the direction of Information not of Implementation
Philosophy
Attitudes to be developed
Policy
purposes
rationale
broad guidelines
Policy
Policy
Policy
Policy
Policy
Schemes of work
Subject
understanding
skills and
processes
Subject
Subject
Subject
Common Learning Processes and Skills
Cross-curricular elements
Teaching and Learning Strategies
including
grouping, resources, assessment, recording ...
Structure
topic/unit/module/theme
Teacher Planning
Implementation
Assessment and Evaluation
• Philosophy and Policies are the responsibility of the governors and must have whole school commitment
• Policy
Some are subject based, others management
More than one policy will inform the component sections of schemes of work
• Schemes of work are the responsibility of the whole staff
• Teacher planning is the responsibility of each teacher
• Assessment will inform/feed back into teacher planning. In particular it informs decisions about differentiation and match, continuity and progression.
• Evaluation will inform/feed back into schemes of work

Figure 7.1

Their first intention was to divide the programmes of study, at Key Stage 2, into manageable chunks for each year group. They agreed to pool ideas about science work that had gone well so that they could offer examples of investigations. Where possible content was linked with other areas of the curriculum.

Main Ideas

Just as Big Ideas have informed the approach in this book so Main Ideas were agreed by the working group at Henleaze as a way of clarifying and identifying the purpose of different parts of the programmes of study and linking activities. What follows is an example.

Main Ideas for Materials and their properties A.T.3

Strand (i): The properties, classification and structure of materials

(1) Materials are natural or manufactured.
(2) The properties of materials determine their use.
(3) Materials can be changed physically.
(4) Materials occur as solids, liquids and gases.

Strand (iii): Chemical changes

(5) Materials can be changed chemically.

Strand (iv): The earth and its atmosphere

(6) Weather studies (recording weather).
(7) Effects of weather.
(8) Study of rocks, minerals and soils.

A similar exercise was undertaken with A.T.s 2 and 4. The group agreed that some of the strands in the A.T.s could be visited on a two year cycle whilst others should be visited each year. The following pattern was agreed:

Visited every year	Visited every two years
A.T.2	
Life processes and the organisation of living things. Populations and human influences within ecosystems.	Variation and the mechanisms of inheritance and evolution. Energy flows and cycles of matter within ecosystems.
A.T.3	
The properties, classification and structure of materials. Explanations of the properties of materials. Chemical changes.	The earth and its atmosphere.
A.T.4	
Energy resources and energy transfer forces and their effects.	Electricity and Magnetism. Light and Sound. The earth's place in the universe.

Using this approach as a framework, each programme of study was divided up between each year to try to ensure that all the content was covered with the minimum of repetition and with built-in progression. The science content was then linked, where possible, to other curriculum areas.

Example of cross-curricular links

Materials and their properties – Year 3

Science	History	Technology
Compare natural and manufactured materials.	Invaders & Settlers.	Design and make clothes using natural and synthetic materials.
Investigate use of materials by	Research use of materials	

'the Invaders & Settlers', for making clothes.
e.g. wool, leather, linen.

Research designs of
clothes.

Devise own fair-tests to
compare
with similar manu-
factured fabrics,
e.g. acrylic, vinyl,
polyester.
e.g. Compare wool and
acrylic.
Test for strength, stretch
wear, etc.
Compare leather and
vinyl.
Test for strength, wear
and flexibility.
Compare linen and
polyester.
Test for strength, wear
and 'creasability'.

| Investigate use of sticks, mud, etc. for building dwellings. | Research designs of dwellings, materials used. | Design and make models of dwellings. |

The Format

Deciding on a format for the scheme was in some ways the most frustrating stage of all for the staff involved. There were several false starts before the following format was finally chosen.

(1)	(2)	(3)	(4)	(5)
Main Ideas	A.T.	Examples of Activities	A.T.1 Skills	Examples of Evidence of Learning

The Main Ideas are in the first column (1) and each activity in column (3) is cross referenced to the relevant main idea. The A.T. column (2) identifies the main A.T. being covered but also indicates, where applicable, other A.T.s which are covered by the activity (see stage 4 – economical activities). Column (3), Examples of Activities, is discussed in detail in stage 4. Column (4), A.T.1 Skills, is included to emphasise the importance of A.T.1. The scientific skills required to carry out each activity were identified and it was intended that this should stress the practical nature of science and, at the same time, act as a guide for teachers in the organisation of their classes and resources. The last column

(5), Examples of Evidence and Learning, was also included as a guide to indicate what children would be expected to produce at the end of each activity, which could then be used as evidence in teacher assessment.

Selecting activities

Selecting activities was the most time-consuming stage of the emerging scheme. Various criteria were used to help identify suitable activities:

(1) They should stand up in their own right as science activities which could be done as part of a subject-based curriculum and not be contrived to fit into topics.
(2) However, where possible they should be 'economical' and have links with other curriculum areas and other science A.T.s
(3) They should ensure continuity.
(4) They should ensure progression.

An attempt to ensure progression was made by selecting some activities within each programme of study which were fairly prescriptive and some which were much more open-ended. These take the exploration stage into the investigative stage, allowing children to work at their own levels in the planning, carrying out and evaluation stages of these activities.

Using these criteria, the final task was to sort through books, workcards, previous lesson plans and the recesses of memory, to come up with enough material.

The Future

As a result of the working group's efforts the school has a science scheme of work which each member of staff is using. It is a working document to be added to as other activities are tried, and the needs of teachers and children change. It constitutes a basis for future developments. It is not regarded by the teachers as a definitive, final or complete document.

Very different decisions were taken by teachers at another school. They concentrated on a direct interpretation of the programmes of study to indicate what *teachers could* do and linked them simply with achievement levels of what *pupils should* be able to do. This planning took place at an early stage of the introduction of the National Curriculum (as may be seen from the numbering of the A.T.s) and represented an attempt to clarify the intentions of the document. Hayley Smith, as science co-ordinator, worked with staff at Summerhill Junior School in Bristol to produce what was for them a manageable working document. The following extract shows how the approach was used:

ATTAINMENT TARGET	USING LIGHT
Pupils should ...	Teachers could ...

LEVEL 1
- know that light comes from different sources

(i) Artificial light.
Provide a collection of light sources, e.g. candles, torches (including coloured torches), light bulbs and batteries. Give children time to handle the materials and to sort them.
Opportunities for testing using candles:
e.g. which candle flame is the brightest? does the size of the candle affect the brightness? does the colour of the candle affect the colour of the flame?

(ii) Natural light.
Draw attention to sunlight and to the effects of the sun:
i.e. how it can cause changes such as:-

a) fading	(e.g. curtains)
b) bleaching	(e.g. hair)
c) browning	(e.g. skin)
d) scorching	(e.g. foliage)
e) burning	(e.g. forest fires)
f) melting	(e.g. tar on roads)

At what time of the year is the sun most powerful? How could we test this? Are these changes/effects of the sun reversible? How can we find out?

(iii) Discuss with pupils light and, dark, day and night, dawn and dusk etc. Encourage observations of natural phenomena, such as: rainbows, lightning, phases of the moon etc.
What ideas do they hold?
Can any of these ideas be tested?

- be able to discriminate between colours and match them or, where appropriate demonstrate an understanding of colour in the environment.

(i) Encourage children, through games and discussions, to observe colours of hair, eyes, clothes they wear etc., and colours of plants and animals in the local environment.

(ii) Ask children to indicate colours that are tones/shades/hues of the *same* colour, e.g. light blue, navy blue etc.

(iii) Make colour collections/corners to highlight awareness of (ii) and develop the concept. Can children invent their own names for certain colours? e.g. 'angry teacher red'. Discussion of evocative names for colours used in advertising; e.g. sanitary ware, cars.

LEVEL 2
- know that light passes through some materials and not others.

Provide a collection of various glass and plastics: some coloured, some transparent, some translucent, and some opaque. Ask children to sort and order the collection in various ways, and to devise a fair test to find out which is the most transparent/opaque.

- and that when it does

not, shadows are formed.

(i) Ask the children to present a story for a shadow puppet theatre.
Use opaque materials and coloured cellophanes.

(ii) Make a human sundial:
i.e. ask children to draw around shadows at different times of the day. (In our climate this may take some time to complete!)

- be able to draw pictures showing features such as light, colour and shade.

Ask children to draw an object in sunlight/in shade/in partial shade etc. using pencils, crayons pastels.

Different schools – different schemes

Where banks of additional information could be useful to staff they may be referenced in the scheme of work. A glut of information could inhibit the early stages of designing a scheme of work: selection therefore needs careful thought. The schemes of work above embody decisions about, revisiting areas of knowledge, longer and shorter-term projects, the pattern over key stages, the balance between Attainment Targets, the way learning will be monitored. The solutions, in each case, are different. The presentation is different. Neither solutions nor presentation can be comprehensive. At any time in a school's history emphasis will be judged appropriate according to need. No scheme or policy can, or could be, all things to all people at all times. That is why they are best decided by individual schools.

Plaintive cries from some perplexed teachers have been heard: 'Just give us a scheme of work and we will do it', (in other words stop this indecision and confusion), 'Tell us exactly what is wanted', (standardise the request and the format so that everyone has the same idea and is doing the same thing), 'Why don't 'they' (the county officers) make up their minds and tell us what to do?' Such requests are inappropriate and most authorities resist responding in absolute terms. Were such requests to be met, the likelihood is that there would then be an outcry about loss of a school's or teacher's individuality and autonomy, about the imposition of doctrine and so on. What is more, if there were a generalised scheme, it could be interpreted so differently that variations would bear little resemblance to the original intentions. At the same time it would kill any original and relevant ways of tackling the task which were suited to individual schools.

The teacher's planning

This is the individual teacher's interpretation of a scheme of work to show precisely how requirements will be met. It is at this point that a teacher develops the main ingredients under the unifying strategy of a topic.

The example in figure 7.2 shows how one school has organised the recording of a teacher's termly planning. A

Science ① Planning Sheet

Topic Time	Duration ½ term	N.C.Year 3/2	Class Teacher Chris Rush	Date 9.92

Main ideas to be covered with A.T.S.

hot/cold   Sc.4.2b

Notes from P-O-S

Talk about when and why they feel hot or cold and link the sensations of hot and cold with thermometer measurements

Activities, including extensions and cross-curricular links where appropriate	Learning Intentions inc. Skills, Concepts, reinforcements and extensions	Assessment/Evidence of Learning
a) Investigate body temperature – discussion. eg. Why do we feel hot/cold? What makes us feel hot/cold? How can we measure it? When do we use a thermometer? When is it important to know the temperature? Link with cooking/freezing/household fuels. (Sc4.3b) extension – children can make lists/sets of hot/cold things	a) children "understand the meaning of hot and cold relative to the temperature of their own bodies. Sc.4.2b eg children able to record hot & cold things in meaningful way	Listen to comments – record relevant statements on child observation sheets annotate work in topic books note original thoughts/observations
b) Use thermometers – small groups. Each child with thermometer. Ensure each child knows how to read it. no some children will read to nearest 5° or 10°, others will read to nearest 1°. Find temperature of the air in the classroom. Record in topic books. Ask children to suggest other things/places to find the temperature of. Can they predict what will happen... eg exam? Can they estimate the temperature? Encourage accurate measurements. Record findings in clear way. extension. Encourage notion of fair-test. Time each reading after 1 minute – children to select way to time 1 minute. Discuss what we found out. Follow any child leads.	b) children able to read thermometer Sc1.3b (to different degrees of accuracy) – able to observe thermometer carefully – able to record findings systematically Sc1.2b - able to suggest something to find the temperature of. Sc1.2a - able to make a prediction. Sc1.3b - giving reasons if possible, discuss what happened. Sc1.2c - able to make a sensible estimation. Ma2.3d - able to measure / record using sensible apparatus (eg stop-watch) Sc1.3c - able ... [children] will be given to explain length of time. Sc1.3c	record what the children say and do on child observation sheets Annotate written work in science/topic book

Where do we go from here	How we could finish the topic	Resources. Cont. over
- Record the temperature, inside/outside the classroom regularly during the year. Record and discuss findings Link to weather/seasons. - School nurse to talk to children about body temperature		collection of thermometers of different types Set of identical thermometers. 1 per child in group.

Figure 7.2

PLANNING SHEET FOR FIRST ACTIVITY			
ACTIVITY	QUESTIONS	PROCESS SKILLS	KNOWLEDGE & UNDERSTANDING
What will the children do? What will they need?	How do you want to lead the activity? What sort of questioning will be appropriate?	What skills will you encourage children to use?	What ideas do you hope children will develop?

Figure 7.3

topic is selected and a web diagram is drawn up by each teacher. The curriculum areas are then specified in a detailed breakdown of what exactly is to be done. The scheme includes the Big Ideas that lie behind the decisions as well as guidance about what will be sought as a check on children's learning.

That there is reference to ways of identifying achievement indicates the beginning of a mechanical link between planning and what the teacher actually learns about the children. The day-to-day evidence which is collected and used for short term planning also informs longer-term planning. (See Chapter 6, pp.166-168, and figure 7.4.)

Day-to-day planning is undertaken, in the first instance, by the teacher who proposes starting points and possible developments for activities. It is then the children who, from their engagement with starting points, help to instigate their own routes towards the Big Ideas, (as illustrated in our case-studies). The starting points could be planned on a sheet as in figure 7.3.

This could show possibilities for investigations and possible illustrative activities. Teachers' notes taken during the early phases of work could be used to indicate direction, (figure 7.4).

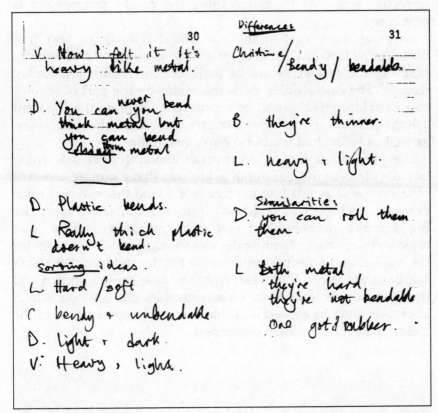

Figure 7.4   J. Thyer: Assessment in Primary Schools Project 1990, N.P.C. (S.W.)

Summary

The purpose of planning is to optimise conditions for learning in the classroom. The factors to be considered are: appropriate areas of study and the relevant accepted scientific interpretations within them; the child's existing framework of ideas and understanding; appropriate starting points for learning; likely avenues of enquiry and investigation; teacher assessment and evaluation; monitoring of progression; required equipment; classroom management. In practice an agreed scheme of work is produced from which individual teachers may select areas of study. The constructivist approach requires that formative teacher-assessment in the classroom, 'loops forward' to inform short-term planning. Thus 'next stages' in a child's learning stand a better chance of being anticipated correctly, while, at the same time, the child's progression is monitored.

What we have tried to show in this chapter is the way that these loops-forward, linking planning decisions to classroom practice, and vice-versa can be built into the teacher's planning records. The case-studies show intentions on the part of schools and individual teachers to be similar but illustrate the different solutions found. Planning is a matter for whole-school decisions as well as individual teachers' implementation.

The proper looping of information about children's learning into decisions in the classroom is the way that planning achieves coherence and avoids fragmentation of a kind that can occur, for example, if a topic web is slavishly pursued for its own sake. The Big Ideas as a way of holding on to significant content whilst using topic webs or other planning devices should provide freedom for the teacher and a proper progression for the children. Whatever solutions are found it is clear, from the case-studies shown and the demands on teachers to be accountable, that a whole school approach must be agreed and that it must be appropriate to the children and the teachers concerned.

CHAPTER 8
Professional Development

1. Introduction

Few would deny that the National Curriculum for Science has made considerable demands upon primary teachers. Many teachers who had not received any specific training in this area of the curriculum or had not previously promoted science within their own classrooms, have had to develop new pedagogical skills – professional knowledge and understanding related to teaching science. For most, this has meant planning, implementing, assessing and evaluating science in a more rigorous way than had been necessary prior to the National Curriculum.

Most teachers have also needed to extend their own knowledge and understanding of the content areas of science included in the National Curriculum. As we noted in Chapter 3, a teacher's understanding of science is essential for assessing children's learning and for making decisions about what to do next. Without an understanding of the content area in which a child is working it is impossible to recognise how a child's existing ideas match or fail to match conventional scientific ideas. This is crucial to deciding how to help the child come to an improved understanding. Without an understanding of the nature of science and scientific processes, it is difficult to support children's attempts to engage in these processes. If a teacher views science as a body of facts to be learnt it is unlikely that children they are teaching will come to understand the tentative nature of scientific ideas.

Teachers engaged in intensive professional development have often gained support from more confident colleagues, sometimes the science co-ordinator, or from someone outside their own school such as an advisory teacher. School-based inservice activities, organised internally or through the LEA support networks, have been common and some teachers have participated in longer centre-based INSET courses, including 20-day DES funded ones, offered by LEAs or Higher Education institutions. Despite this level of activity, there is still a need for further development. Few of us involved in education ever feel confident enough about our professional practice to suggest there is no room for improvement. Enlightened teachers constantly evaluate their classroom work and try out new strategies and approaches.

This chapter encourages the use of a systematic process for introducing and evaluating new approaches and ideas. It is a process that encourages teachers to reflect critically on what already goes on in their classrooms, to propose ways of modifying their practice in order to improve children's learning, and to evaluate new approaches rigorously by testing out their value in the classroom. It is based on the premise that decisions about the success of a new way of working should be based on evidence, not impressions. For this reason, it is an approach that requires teachers to collect evidence of what is happening in their classroom and to be able to analyse that evidence in order to evaluate whether a particular approach is achieving its purpose. This process is often referred to as 'action research'.

The chapter draws upon the experience of many teachers who have become reflective practitioners and have learnt to make decisions about their future action as a result of that reflection. Action research can be a form of educational research that is firmly based in the classroom and in which teachers are in full control of their own professional development. It can also be used to address educational concerns beyond the classroom such as those related to school management and teacher-appraisal. Action research can be used by anyone involved in education including students, new entrants to the profession, experienced teachers, headteachers, advisory teachers, advisers and college tutors.

As a result of becoming researchers in their own classrooms many teachers have come to appreciate the benefits of collaboration with colleagues. We authors have been involved in a number of projects in which we have facilitated and encouraged such collaboration and examples of these are offered to indicate the advantages. Put simply, 'two heads are better than one' and the discussion of classroom experiences provides new insights into professional practice which can be genuinely useful in helping individuals construct a better understanding of how science might be taught. The National Curriculum has undoubtedly encouraged teachers to work together more closely in terms of planning and so a foundation already exists; such collaboration can now be extended to improve what actually happens in the classroom when plans are put into action. There are ways in which work with colleagues can be formalised and a case-study is used to illustrate how a confident teacher, in this case a co-ordinator, can support less confident members of staff.

The potential benefits of INSET activities initiated from outside the school context are considerable, particularly in the area of professional development related to teachers' subject knowledge. Distance-learning materials can also be valuable for those teachers who prefer to work more independently. This aspect of professional development is addressed in the final section of the chapter.

2. What is action research?

Educational action research is a systematic and rigorous process for enabling teachers to deal with concerns that they have about their professional practice. Action research has its origins in the work of Lewin (1946) but its educational potential has been explored more recently by Stenhouse (1975) and others (Schon, 1983; Ebbutt and Elliot, 1985; Hopkins, 1985; McNiff, 1988; Elliot, 1991). It has developed as a way of making research more meaningful to teachers. There is, traditionally, a view of educational research as something done by outside researchers, who carry out large scale projects in classrooms, generalise their findings and then tell teachers how they can improve their practice. Dissemination of this kind of research rarely has the impact in classrooms that its advocates desire. Teachers have no ownership of the research and are therefore often not sufficiently motivated to make changes, especially when those changes may involve considerable effort and anguish.

Action research has much more limited aims. It is concerned with teachers finding specific solutions to particular problems which have arisen in their individual classrooms. Unlike some research approaches, action research does not set out to generate generalisations. For example, a teacher may have a concern about the involvement of girls in practical work. This concern is, perhaps, most appropriately seen as a question, 'How can I ensure the girls in my class get more involved in practical work?'. The emphasis of the 'I' (Whitehead and Barrett, 1985) reinforces the personal nature of the concern, although others may, of course, share similar concerns about their own practice. Teachers, as researchers, set out to find better ways of working in their own situation but it may be that successful strategies will work for others and making findings public at some stage may be desirable. However, teachers' immediate purpose in engaging in the research process is to address their own concerns and not to find generalised truths for others to take on. Indeed, many action researchers write up their work in order to encourage others to engage in the same process, rather than as an attempt to offer guidance to someone else about teaching.

So what is the process? This question will probably generate as many answers as there are teachers engaging in action research. At its simplest, it is a process which begins with a concern that a teacher has identified, perhaps with the help of someone else. This concern is then thought about and possible ways of addressing it are considered. This stage may well involve eliciting the views of others in an attempt to gain new perspectives on the problem. One of the resultant proposed solutions is then turned into some form of action plan. The action plan will need to involve consideration of how the teacher will be able to decide whether or not the strategy has been successful. In other words, before trying something out, the teacher will decide what evidence, or data, to collect in order that the outcome can be evaluated. The next stage involves implementing the proposal in the classroom. This is when data is collected. Relevant data may be a record of the teacher's utterances or those of the children. It may involve recording the teacher's own actions, observing children's behaviours or collecting their work. Following a period of classroom work, the data has to be analysed. This is the stage of reflecting upon what occurred in order to gain insights into the success or otherwise of the new strategy. Analysis is difficult and can be time consuming. To be valuable it needs to be rigorous and honest. In research terms it should be valid and stand up to the examination of someone else's scrutiny. Does the evidence support the statements a teacher is making about a classroom episode? It is at this stage that collaboration with a colleague, or group of colleagues, is essential. Trying out one's ideas and testing the conclusions drawn from the evidence against the professional views of others can be made less threatening if conducted in a climate of mutual respect and support. It is unlikely that this analysis and reflection will result in the teacher feeling that the concern has been finally resolved. In the 'messiness' of real classroom situations the likely outcome will be a refined concern or perhaps a new concern and a revised action plan. Action research involves a cyclical process in which evaluation leads to new action. We are talking about increasingly fine tuning to a classroom need, rather like finding a station on a radio dial.

To ensure that decisions about teaching are based on evidence of what actually happens rather than on impressions it is vital that evidence is collected in a systematic way. It is in this area that the teacher as researcher can draw profitably on more conventional research methods. Data can be collected in a variety of ways including: field notes (written during or straight after the session); tape recording; videotaping; pupil diaries or work; interviews; questionnaires; sociometry; photography (Hopkins, 1985). It is obviously desirable for data to be as objective as possible, but it is equally obvious that no classroom data is totally objective. There can be great value in subjective teacher views and in teachers' interpretations of particular situations. Action research is rarely concerned with exclusively quantitative methods and issues related to sampling, control groups and careful control of all variables, are less important than in other forms of research. It is a qualitative approach to research in which an individual teacher is attempting to build up as accurate a picture of what goes on in a child's mind as is necessary for making decisions about classroom approaches. It is, by definition, a form of educational research which impacts on a teacher's professional practice.

3. Why engage in action research?

What are the features of action research that make it particularly suitable for teachers? Perhaps, most significantly, it is a spur to action. It is a means of getting something done and improving the way in which it is done. In this sense, it is a tool for teachers' own problem-solving which is a preferable alternative to the more subjective and impressionistic approach to problem-solving often used in education. Because it is open-ended and flexible it can be adapted to suit the style of any teacher and may be used in any teaching context.

Engaging in action research does more than just change practice; it adds to teachers' working knowledge of that practice. As researchers, teachers can gain new and valuable insights into how they go about teaching. Action research helps teachers make their own value systems more explicit and helps overcome the distance between 'espoused theories', which teachers use in order to talk about what they say they do and think they do, and 'theories in action' which reflect what actually goes on in their classrooms (Easen, 1985: 6). In enabling teachers to examine the extent to which their values are represented in their practice it throws light on classroom relationships and the behaviour of both children and teachers. It helps us to know ourselves better as professionals. In Schon's term, we develop 'knowledge-in-action' (1983, p.50).

Action research leads to innovation, especially if it involves the collaborative dimension. However, to achieve such innovation the teachers involved must approach their research in an open-minded way, prepared to be self-critical and recognising that they can learn from others. To be successful, it is also important for teacher-researchers to appreciate that their research activity is not something they 'do' to their practice. It should be seen as inextricably linked with practice, a natural part of it. Accepting and evaluating the perceptions of colleagues is something which competent teachers do as a matter of course.

4. What does a teacher need in order to engage in action research?

As noted, an openness to new perspectives is essential for any teacher-researcher, but there are other qualities and skills that are desirable. Teachers wishing to improve their practice have to make a personal commitment to achieving that improvement; someone else cannot do it for them. In the same way that children must actively construct their scientific understanding of the world, teachers must actively construct an understanding of their own professional practice. To raise concerns about one's own practice requires a degree of curiosity, honesty and confidence. For many of us, the values upon which our practice is based remain implicit. Raising concerns requires those values, and the dilemmas we face every day as teachers, to be highlighted in order that they may be identified and diagnosed.

A teacher-researcher needs to be creative, to think of new ways of doing things which can be tried out. During the implementation of these new ideas a teacher needs to have appropriate observation skills; to be an active listener and responsive questioner. It is not as easy as one might imagine to observe one's own practice. Looking closely at what goes on demands we are alert to all sorts of implicit and explicit cues (Rowland, 1984). When data has been collected the teacher needs to be able to analyse it critically and this demands a degree of integrity. Many teacher-researchers find the act of writing up their own research is itself a valuable part of the process. Stenhouse talks about 'systematic enquiries made public' (1975) and in the introduction to this chapter it was implied that colleagues may find individuals' insight into their own practice useful in providing a different perspective. Action-researchers, then, also need to be able to manufacture time in which to undertake the process. However, along with many of the teachers we have worked with, we have found that the simple act of writing up case-studies can help clarify our ideas and so even this minimal gesture can be well worth the time and effort it requires.

5. What concerns can a teacher address through action research?

Whenever we work in an educational context we inevitably face a complex set of dilemmas (Pollard and Tann, 1987, p.5). Resolving these dilemmas can, according to Whitehead, lead to our personal educational values being denied (Whitehead and Barrett, 1985). These dilemmas can relate to the relationships we have within the classroom, the way in which the classroom is managed and organised, the nature of the curriculum we offer children and how we put that curriculum into action. Within the context of science some of these dilemmas might be:

- Should I organise science as a whole-class, group or individual activity?
- Should I control the direction of the activity, the use of time and resources or allow the children to take control?
- Should I plan scientific activities based on children's interests or on National Curriculum requirements?
- Should I encourage children to explore one scientific area in depth or attempt to provide a broad coverage of all areas?
- Should I focus on skills or knowledge and understanding in a particular activity?
- Should the fostering of attitudes be given a high priority or are skills more important?
- Which children should be learning to work co-operatively and which developing self-reliance at this particular moment?
- Should I give all children equal time or focus on those with particular needs?
- Should I give the children answers or ask them more questions?

These concerns are, of course, not intended to imply mutual exclusivity; for example, work on scientific skills does not preclude the development of scientific ideas. The concerns do, however, offer a range of areas in which teachers might focus their attention. In all of these areas every single teacher is required to make professional decisions which will affect the quality of children's learning in science. In none of these areas is there a simple 'right' answer. The resolution of each dilemma will depend upon the particular circumstances and social context in which an individual teacher works. For that reason the way forward must be for teachers to address the concern in their own individual way. The framing of each question in the first person is significant because, to ensure commitment to its resolution, the individual must feel it is his or her own concern, that they have ownership of it and a vested interest in resolving it. In some respects the use of the word 'concern' could imply a negative dimension. Our view is that we should see concerns in a more positive way. A desire to improve does not necessarily mean something is 'wrong' with what we already do in our classrooms.

Most of the questions formulated above are couched in fairly general terms. Others may be more tightly formulated. Examples of more tightly focused concerns are:

- Am I listening to children's responses during whole class discussions and responding appropriately?
- Am I allowing children enough exploration time before encouraging them to engage in investigative work?
- What strategies can I use to get the children raising more scientific questions?
- How can I elicit the existing ideas of less confident children during group discussions?
- Do the girls get a fair share of the discussion time available?

Having identified a concern, it is necessary to diagnose the contributory features of the concern and to postulate ways of improving the situation.

The following case-study illustrates a teacher's approach to addressing a concern related to children's self-assessment. It provides an interesting comparison with the case-study in Chapter 6 in which Jan Isaac addressed a similar concern in a different way. Both teachers adopted a systematic approach to their classroom enquiries and found ways of improving their practice. The case-study is from Pat Haywood of Longvernal Primary School, Midsomer Norton. It is a written account of several weeks' work.

CASE-STUDY: SELF-ASSESSMENT

As a Y3 teacher, Pat recognised that, 'learning is greatly improved when pupils and teachers are clear about what they have done, what they have grasped and where they are going next'. She considered self-assessment to be vital to a child's learning and formulated a concern, 'How can I support the children's self-assessment?'.

The first phase of her research involved diagnosing the present situation in her classroom. Her exploratory observations of what was happening included some tape-recording of her discussions with children, individually and in small groups. She had been confident that she had a 'language-rich classroom, in which there were many opportunities for children to discuss their work and to learn from and bounce ideas off each other'. However, she was made aware from listening to the tapes that the children were answering questions 'in the way in which they think their teacher expects them to'. She felt that 'if they are encouraged to reflect on their work and discuss their progress, they may gain more confidence in themselves and be less likely to be afraid to give 'wrong' answers'. She was aware of the significance of children's alternative ideas in science and was therefore keen to encourage children to share the ideas they held, rather than the ones they thought the teacher wanted to hear. Her analysis of one of the discussions she taped, in which the children were discussing their work on forces, provided evidence of 'one child, Sam, who became aware that her understanding was inadequate and evidently wished to end the discussion as quickly as possible. She started answering questions curtly with "Don't know", and provided no further amplification of her understanding'.

Pat talked to her colleagues as she considered ways of addressing the concern. In one of the staff-room books she read about the use of a sentence completion exercise as part of a review or 'de-briefing' discussion and decided to try this out. She felt that 'the "fun" element of such an exercise, if introduced as a game, might encourage the children to feel less self-conscious and provide an opportunity for the most reticent children to voice their opinions'. She modified the idea she had read about and formulated some sentence beginnings:

> The things I enjoyed about the work were . . .
> I discovered that . . .
> I learnt that . . .
> I found . . . . . difficult to do because . . .
> I think I could improve if . . .
> I would like to find out . . .
> I don't understand . . .
> I know that . . .
> I didn't like . . .

These were written on strips of card. A group of four children were invited to play the 'game', having completed a session of exploratory activities with simple circuit equipment. The teacher left the group alone but taped their discussion. Each child took it in turns to take a card from the pile and then one at a time the whole group completed the sentence orally.

When Pat analysed the contents of the tape it provided evidence that enabled her to evaluate the strategy both in terms of the children's increasing confidence in their own ideas and in terms of evidence of the children's learning. Her analysis concluded:

> All of the group offered responses without much hesitation, apart from the sentences referring to 'I think I could improve if ...' and 'I would like to find out ...'. However, some were obviously influenced by what they had heard others say. The vocabulary used, and the way it was used, showed that two of the children had begun to understand some of the new concepts involved in the activity. They used the terms 'circuit', 'conductors' and 'flow' appropriately, e.g. 'Metal things are conductors and worked in my circuit', 'The bulb only works when electricity can flow around the circuit'. The other two were using similar terms but without the same level of understanding evident, e.g. 'I learned about electricity and bulbs lighting up', and 'I learned the circuit bulb only lighted sometimes'. The self-assessment highlighted some organisation problems since it was evident that 'waiting for a screwdriver' had proved a problem. The difficulties they all noted about connecting wires to components may have been avoided if I had provided more crocodile clips.

Pat was satisfied that the 'game' had encouraged responses from all the children and the tendency to provide the answer the teacher wanted to hear was not evident. However, her non-involvement with the group had meant some utterances, which might have been significant, were not probed. She was also disturbed that the children were not showing much curiosity about 'what they would like to find out'. The first of these points was obviously related to her initial concern and led to a revised action plan. She used the cards again, with another group and asked them to write down their ideas in a 'think book' (see Chapter 3). When she joined the group she used this written record to probe individuals' ideas further, where it was necessary. The other insight from the analysis of evidence collected, concerning the children's lack of curiosity, opened a slightly different direction of enquiry, which had not been part of in the initial concern but which she considered deserved further attention.

Pat believed that, as a teacher, she should be enabling children to assess their own achievements. Having explored her concern she proposed a solution, effectively a working hypothesis, which deserved to be tested out in practice. She implemented her solution in a systematic manner having decided that evidence from a tape-recording of the children's discussion would allow her to evaluate the appropriateness of her strategy. She critically analysed what happened in order to decide what further action was necessary. In doing this she identified a related concern which also deserved attention.

This raises an issue that is constantly debated by action researchers. Should an enquiry remain focused on one key concern, or, when new concerns arise, should they also be addressed? It might be argued that, in one sense, as soon as teachers identify a concern they cannot help but make professional decisions informed by that new knowledge. However, that is different from using the new concern as a focus for further classroom enquiry. McNiff (1988) offers a form of action research which she calls 'generative'. This recognises that teachers will be dealing with several different concerns at once, although at different levels of intensity. She views the action research process as a spiral which generates smaller peripheral spirals of related concerns. She claims that these other concerns can be 'explored as and when they arise without the researcher losing sight of the main focus of the enquiry' (p.45).

The process in which Pat engaged was cyclic. Although the case-study only discusses the first cycle, she subsequently tried out several different strategies for encouraging the children in their self-assessment. She wrote up her experience to share with a group of teachers with whom she was working as part of an INSET course. In this way she clarified her new understanding of her own professional practice and provided an opportunity for others to learn from her experience. There was nothing particularly profound about what she did or discovered, but, in the context of her own particular situation, it led to improved learning opportunities in science for her children and enabled her to make her practice more accurately represent her educational values. Such action is indicative of professional competence.

6. Why collaborate?

There are many ways in which teachers can collaborate and indeed already do. The extent to which the National Curriculum has required whole school planning has been discussed in Chapter 7. More detailed collaborative planning in science is also common in many primary schools, particularly where classes are team-taught or in year-groups or units. The benefits of such planning in terms of efficiency are obvious. Some teachers also evaluate collaboratively, although in many situations such discussions tend to be based on impressions of what was or was not successful rather than discussions on evidence of what actually happened. Individual teachers can and do collect such evidence and, more frequently now, teachers are discussing their assessment decisions, based on evidence of children's learning, during moderation meetings.

The advantages of evaluating teaching practice reciprocally with a colleague in the classroom are less commonly recognised and staffing constraints in primary schools mean opportunities for such collaboration can be limited. However, where such opportunities are exploited the rewards can be enormous for all concerned. Such initiatives need both partners to feel they are collaborating in a secure and non-judgemental atmosphere and this needs sensitive handling.

Our experiences of facilitating collaborative activities in the classroom have led us to favour a model in which planning, teaching, and evaluation are reflexive, with both partners taking it in turns to teach and observe, coming together to plan improved versions of the practice and then swapping roles again. We have also come to recognise the particular benefits of enabling a pair to focus their attention on a small group of not more than four to six children (Ritchie 1989; 1991c; Ollerenshaw and Ritchie, 1990; Ollerenshaw et al., 1991). This allows the observer to record most of the teacher's and children's utterances and actions, so that the pair's subsequent analysis of an episode is based on the most accurate picture of what happened, that it is practical to record.

Although it is expensive it is desirable, but not essential, for another adult to be in the room to supervise the rest of the class. In any event, the observer should not be required to take on a supervisory role, but it is possible for the one whose turn it is to teach to supervise the rest whilst focusing on one group. Classroom teachers rarely have the opportunity to look closely at aspects of their practice and reflect upon the implications of what they see. To quote T.S. Eliot:

> We had the experience, but missed the meaning,
> And approach to the meaning restores the experience
> In a different form ...'
> (Four Quartets)

Such an experience for a teacher can be an extremely revealing one and have a profound influence on the individual concerned. It can highlight significant aspects of teaching and of children's learning which remain unnoticed in the normal classroom situation.

If a school staff recognises the potential of such collaboration there are ways in which it can be organised without too much disruption. It is, of course, possible to use school funds to release a teacher and provide cover. This is expensive, and within the limited budgets of a small school, unlikely. There are, however, other less expensive ways. Most primary schools are flexible and it is possible to use certain times in the day creatively to release a teacher. Assemblies, story-times, TV time and singing practice all have potential for freeing a teacher. In many schools headteachers provide time for teachers to be freed from class responsibilities for a limited period and this time can be used to work in a colleague's class. Another way of facilitating collaboration is to use an inservice day and arrange for pairs of teachers to work with a small group of children.

It is important for teachers to be clear about why they are working with a small group in such an intense way in order to avoid the response, 'This is so unrealistic; it has got no relevance to my ordinary teaching'. It is, of course, impractical to collect such comprehensive evidence during ordinary classroom work. The purpose of working in such an atypical way is to enable teachers to focus on their practice with a small group, or even an individual, in order to understand the nature of their interaction with children and to develop skills and improve their 'editing' capabilities which can then be used effectively in the normal classroom situation. Such experiences can have particular benefits in developing teachers' assessment skills (see Chapter

6). The opportunity to analyse teaching episodes in detail can help teachers to develop skills of responsive questioning and active listening which can be applied in the normal classroom context when assessing children's learning.

This approach to developing teacher assessment skills was developed during a collaborative project in which the authors were involved and it resulted in an INSET package (Ollerenshaw et al., 1991) which has been used extensively in primary schools and also by the authors during DES Science courses which are discussed later in this chapter. The value of collaborative work in classrooms as a means of professional development in primary science has also been recognised by the Science Teacher Action Research (STAR) Project and was used extensively to develop assessment skills of teachers involved in the project (Cavendish et al., 1990: 10). The team found the teachers involved and, encouragingly, their children, benefited from collaborative work.

The following case-study illustrates collaboration between two teachers, Wendy Davey and Neil Tuttiett, who worked in the same rural primary school – Mary Elton Primary School in Avon – and shared a common concern about the role of girls in their science activities. Their initial focus was to look at what was going on, within pairs and small groups, when teacher involvement was minimal, in order to discover whether the children listened to each other and changed their opinions in the light of what others said. Their intention, after this exploratory phase, was to explore teaching strategies to facilitate the further active involvement of girls in science and technological work. As a result of LEA support they were able to spend a number of sessions working collaboratively and to discuss their findings with an advisory teacher who acted as a commentator during analysis and evaluation of classroom episodes. They collected data in their classrooms using field notes, photography and audio-tape recording. They collaboratively planned activities and alternated the role of teacher and observer.

The following extract from a summary report, written by these two teachers, draws upon their collaborative analysis of data and the resulting discussions. It provides an indication of the insights the teachers gained into the children's thinking as they attempted to add a working light to a model room they had constructed. The Y4 children involved had chosen their own pairings.

CASE-STUDY: GROUP DYNAMICS WITH MINIMAL TEACHER-INVOLVEMENT

Samantha and Matthew – Samantha sat back and let Matthew handle the equipment. At the planning stage they had worked together well, talking about ideas, although Matthew did not change his ideas whereas Samantha did. Samantha expressed the opinion that she knew less. Matthew beavered away with the problem as Samantha sat at his side. She 'chipped in' with ideas but was content to let Matthew attempt most of the work. Samantha eventually started playing with a set of magnets instead of trying to solve the problem. Samantha said to the teacher, about Matthew's idea to use some construction equipment, 'We're going to use Lego but I don't normally play with this stuff'.

Christopher and Kelly – Christopher was very much in charge in this pairing. He kept much of the equipment on his side of the table, thus keeping Kelly away from it. Kelly remained in the background throughout, but maintained her interest in the task and attempted to break his monopoly. Christopher became quite frustrated at one point when he could not make the light come on every time. Peter and Eve had solved this problem early on which made him even more frustrated. At one stage he went over to the other group to find out how they had managed it. Kelly came up with a practical suggestion to solve the problem and explained herself well, but Christopher ignored it. After a while he called Peter over to look at the problem. Peter made a few suggestions which Christopher accepted without question. Christopher was asked by Wendy (who was adopting the teaching role), why he was changing his idea, to which he replied, 'Because Peter told me to'. 'Will it (Peter's idea) make it better?'. Christopher replied 'I don't know'. At one stage Christopher said to Kelly: 'Trust you! The whole thing has fallen apart'. Kelly occasionally lost interest, but when she was allowed to participate she did enjoy some success. Even though the light was not working properly, Christopher wanted to fit a buzzer but could not make it work. Kelly knew how to operate the buzzer but she was refused use of the battery. She got another one to demonstrate but again Christopher took it from her. Eventually Christopher produced a working model that contained many of Kelly's ideas, though he had not accepted them from Kelly but from his friend.

Wendy intentionally did not intervene with the dynamics of the pair during this activity. We were quite shocked by how far Christopher was prepared to go, and the strategies he employed, to keep Kelly in the background.

Peter and Eve worked together right from the start. They co-operatively determined the course of the action to take. Eve explained her plan to Peter, then Peter explained his plan in return. Eve decided that Peter's plan was less complicated than her own and they both decided to work from Peter's idea. They worked in harmony – sometimes with four hands on the task. At one point, they tried to saw a piece of wood in half, each sawing half way through the wood!

Wendy and Neil were concerned about whether the children were listening to each other and changing their minds as a result of what others were saying. Their initial observations suggested this was only evident in one pairing and in the others the girls were taking a minimal role in decision-making and activity and their ideas, often sound, were being ignored by more dominant partners. These exploratory findings disturbed both teachers since they had not been aware of such dominant and aggressive behaviour in group situations. They resolved to explore strategies to improve children's co-operative skills.

The second session

Neil took over the teaching role for the next session, a week later, based on the same task but with a new group. At the beginning of the session he stressed the need for co-operation, consideration and the need to listen to each other. This group decided to work together rather than in pairs. Wendy and Neil's account continues:

They assembled the electric circuit equipment and took time discussing what they would do. Jane was extremely quiet and at one stage the teacher said 'I wonder what Jane thinks' and the others answered, almost in unison, 'Jane hasn't spoken at all!'. Jane's contribution at that point was not particularly significant. However, a little later, as the group were pursuing

Robert's idea that they needed to put a chain of paper clips around the box, and were engrossed in so doing, Jane said 'I don't think we need paper clips at all'. This was ignored. The teacher intervened and said 'Did you hear what Jane said? Please say it again, Jane'. She repeated and the other group members said 'Oh no! We don't really, do we!' and they then proceeded to ask her how she would do it. They then accepted this proposal and the final, quite simple but functional, model was nearest to Jane's original plan. '

It was evident that Neil's intervention, although minimal, had influenced and modified the children's behaviour within the group. Drawing attention to Jane's statement changed the whole design of the model. Was it because the group valued Jane's idea or because it must be a good idea if the teacher has drawn attention to it?

The two teachers concluded that the teacher intervention to combat dominant children not listening to ideas from less dominant children had worked in this instance. However, further analysis of Neil's interactions during this session led to the conclusion that whatever he said to the children, they seemed to be looking for hidden meanings and clues as to their performance and the acceptability of their ideas. This became the focus of the teachers' next session when they decided to make it explicit to the children that they wanted them to think for themselves as well as listening to others. Wendy, who led the next sessions, which involved the original group, stressed that there was not a right answer and they should try and co-operate with each other, listen to what other people had to say and share out jobs. The task involved finding the best way to join materials, in the context of making a bag. Wendy and Neil decided to observe whether the male domination that had been noticed during the previous session was modified following the teacher emphasis on co-operation and also to see if the handling of fabrics/needles/cotton as opposed to circuit equipment gave the girls more confidence.

Summary of the third session

Samantha and Matthew – At the beginning of the session, Samantha was much more confident and discussed with Matthew how to join using buttons and threads. She soon started to lose her confidence, however, when handling the materials. Samantha: 'I bet it will end up like last time when we didn't finish'. After this Matthew took the materials and tried to sew them together. He soon lost interest and Samantha took over the sewing again. Matthew took another two pieces of material and stuck them together with tape and paper fasteners. Matthew made it clear he thought it was a girl's activity. Samantha tried to assert herself by referring to the need to sew a zip with the use of a running stitch. When Samantha offered advice to Matthew, 'If you put those two together like that . . .', Matthew's retort was, 'That's just what I said!'. It seemed to us that he was unwilling to accept that any good idea Samantha offered was her own.

Kelly and Christopher – Christopher began working by himself trying to join pieces of fabric using paper fasteners. When Matthew asked Kelly if she could sew and got an affirmative answer, he said, 'Oh good, you'll be alright then, Chris'. As a result of this Christopher began consulting Kelly more, but she was more interested in looking at the others. Only when Wendy suggested he let Kelly try her idea did she become actively involved.

Eve and Peter – Initially Peter sat back, with Eve holding the needle and joining the material. However they soon reverted to 'the old routine' of co-operating, even to the extent of one of them holding the material while the other pushed the needle through. Eve was concerned that Peter hadn't held the needle and said: 'Do you want to have a go at sewing?', to which he replied, 'No I can't do it as well as you'.

At the end of the session Wendy asked all the pairs if they felt they had shared the task. They all thought they had. The boys seemed rather thrown by the part sewing played in the activity. They were reluctant to actually sew. We thought the girls would be at an advantage and that this might have a bearing on the group dynamics. In the first two pairs, however, we felt the boys were still effectively, 'driving from the back seat'.

By this time, Wendy and Neil had observed children's co-operation very closely on three occasions and were beginning to develop some new insights into their practice. They summarise their findings in this way:

208

We did not really want to believe that the boys were pushing the girls out of these types of activities but we were increasingly aware that this is a problem and quite a serious one. We were also quite surprised at the lengths children will go to to please the teacher. This 'need' will sometimes override all reason and original thought. Children showed that they believe everything the teacher says or does (related to 'work') and will constantly look for teacher clues as to the 'right answer', the clues being in any form – a nod, a wink, smile, hand gesture, or instruction. They seem to feel insecure with an 'open-ended answer'.

We feel we have gained important insights into the behaviour of groups. Far more goes on in the classroom than we had previously noticed that affects the well-being and education of the child. This has illustrated to us the 'power' of group dynamics and that as teachers we need to give much thought to the groupings of children within the class. This has implications for the whole curriculum. Girls seemed happy to get actively involved in, and in some cases control, group discussion but when it came to practical work the boys took over and this needed sensitive teacher intervention.

These teachers had been given the opportunity to work collaboratively and develop a shared understanding of their work with children. The use of words like 'shocked' and 'disturbed' provides evidence of how revealing such close observation of groups can be for the individuals concerned. However, both recognised that as a result of what they did they are now different teachers, with an increased awareness of the nature of the social context in which they teach, and the effect that group dynamics can have on learning. They have gained a new personal insight into their role in relation to those dynamics.

Their early exploratory work became a starting point for subsequent classroom enquiries that are continuing two years after the advisory teacher support ended.

7. Supporting less confident colleagues

Most primary schools now have a co-ordinator for science and a part of this role is to support colleagues in their attempts to implement science in their classrooms. This support can take many forms, including assistance with planning; the provision of appropriate resources and equipment; advice about using particular resources; advice about classroom organisation and management; information about new developments; help for children with special education needs; advice on integrating the use of IT into science work; advice on assessment and record-keeping. All of this support can be useful and valuable. However, in our experience the most effective support in terms of changing daily practice involves working alongside a teacher. In this the school's science co-ordinator adopts a role common in advisory teacher work and for that reason it is appropriate to look at some evidence of the success of that role.

Harland (1990) carried out a detailed evaluation of science advisory teachers' work in an attempt to highlight successful strategies. He identified four distinct modes of working which can be related to the role of co-ordinators working in their own schools. The first mode was *provisionary* and involved giving teachers materials and physical resources; it was the 'I will give you what you need' approach. The second was called the *hortative* mode and involved the 'I will encourage and tell you how to improve your practice' approach. The next mode was described as *role modelling* and involved the advisory teacher in showing a teacher 'how to do it'. The fourth was the *zetetic* mode and it involved advisory teachers in supporting teachers in critically examining their existing practice. It was essentially a 'let us enquire together' approach which required the advisory teacher to help the class teacher identify a concern. This led to the advisory teacher becoming a 'critical friend'.

The provisionary mode had obvious advantages but it proved difficult to move away from this role if that was where the support started. Such a role did not address fundamental questions about how resources should be used. The hortative mode was appreciated by teachers but found to be of limited value if not supported by other strategies. Similarly the role modelling mode was appreciated at the time but had limited long-term impact on practice, particularly where it led to uncritical and behaviouristic imitations of the approach demonstrated. Again, it was seen to have some value but, ideally, only as part of a variety of approaches used with a teacher. The zetetic mode proved very successful when it worked but was a high risk strategy which sometimes failed. It was found vital for the

210

individuals involved to share qualities like tolerance, openness and a willingness to share uncertainties.

Overall, it was found desirable for support to be offered in a variety of modes, in response to the particular needs of the teacher concerned. There were other factors identified which affected the outcome of the support. These could again be related to the role of the co-ordinator and included the enthusiasm, skills and credibility of the supporter. Success was also dependent upon support over a sustained period, appropriate diagnosis of an individual's needs, time to talk, the degree of support and commitment from the headteacher, a school culture that was conducive to change and the availability of resources.

The following case-study illustrates a co-ordinator working with a colleague and provides evidence of some of the above factors being addressed. It describes the initial stages of a programme of support which lasted several months, with the co-ordinator gradually reducing the level of support available. The co-ordinator herself was also gaining support during this work from another co-ordinator at a school in the local cluster group and limited opportunities were available for both co-ordinators to work in the same school; this was a factor in the success of the support.

CASE-STUDY: THE ROLE OF SCIENCE CO-ORDINATOR

The co-ordinator, Jill Spiteri, of Whitchurch Primary School in Bristol, had, in negotiation with her headteacher, identified a colleague with whom to start the programme of support. This decision was based on the criterion that the colleague would be open to new ideas and prepared to try out new strategies in her classroom. It was also decided that the individual should be prepared to share with other colleagues in staff meetings what was happening and its impact in her classroom.

There are, of course, difficulties about this approach to identifying staff if the individual concerned is not interested or cooperative. Colleagues who identify their own professional need for support are much more likely to be committed to developing their practice.

The teacher chosen, Anna, was a reception teacher who, when approached, was very keen, fortunately. The general assistant who worked several mornings a week in Anna's class was also invited to become involved. The aim of the support was initially to develop the colleague's keenness for, and confidence in, tackling practical scientific work. It was then hoped that opportunities would arise to develop Anna's own knowledge and understanding of science through ongoing support and guidance.

Identifying needs

Work with an individual colleague should always start with an identification of that person's perceived professional needs.

Anna was in her second year of teaching, having spent her first year in a nursery class. She admitted in initial discussions to 'being nervous about science'. She considered it something complicated that she had not been good at as a pupil and said, 'It frightens me; I found it hard and so I think my children will'. When asked more specifically what support she wanted she replied, 'Anything to get me going!'. Through more focused questioning her needs were defined as:

(i)   How to begin activities: 'Even after looking in books on primary science I can't help thinking, how do I get this going?'
(ii) How can I make the best use of children's books and resources?
(iii) How can I possibly assess children's science?
(iv) What do I do about the science I don't know?'

Choosing a strategy

Jill, through discussion with Anna and her fellow co-ordinator (from within the cluster group) recognised that it was important to make a supportive and gentle start in order to 'engender an enthusiasm for science in someone whose self-esteem related to the subject was low'. The two co-ordinators had had the opportunity to work collaboratively with a group of children as part of an INSET activity they attended through the LEA. This had involved collaborative planning, an initial teaching session during which one of the pair observed, a collaborative analysis of the session and planning for a second session during which roles were reversed. They had both found this activity useful

212

and decided to replicate it in their own schools.

Jill explained to Anna, during an after-school discussion, what was involved. She offered to teach a small group for the first session whilst Anna observed and collected data. They collaboratively planned an activity for a group based on the topic of clothes that Anna was following with her class. They decided that, after analysis and evaluation of the first session, Anna would teach a modified version of the same activity to a different group. The general assistant, who was also involved in the discussion, would work with the rest of the class on activities that had been set up by Anna, and keep a watching brief on the science group.

Anna had made limited use of collections previously and therefore Jill suggested a collection of fabrics would be a good starting point. She had used fabrics before and thought they would immediately capture the children's interest and provide plenty of opportunities for observations, sorting, identifying similarities and differences and raising questions. The work was to be exploratory with the children being encouraged to use all of their senses. Anna was invited to choose the children and included Luke for the first session because he was usually unresponsive in class. She warned Jill about this but felt it would be useful for her, as his class teacher, to see how he responded in a small group situation with intensive adult support. Jill introduced Anna to the idea of a floor-book as a means of recording the children's ideas and questions.

Putting plans into action

The two sessions took place on the same day, either side of a lunch-break, made longer than usual by the headteacher's offer to read the class a story. After school the pair spent more time analysing what had happened and discussing the issues that arose about teachers' questions and assessment.

Evaluating the support

The following questions were agreed by Jill and her fellow co-ordinator as appropriate to help them evaluate the first phase of the support:

(a) What aspects of the sessions were you pleased about?

(b) What aspects of the sessions were you unhappy about?
(c) To what extent have your needs been fulfilled?
(d) What aspects of the work could you take further with the children?
(e) What further collaboration would be desirable?

Anna's comments at the end of the day indicated that she had gained much from being able to observe Jill working with a group in her class. She commented that the collection was 'a practical starting point that worked'. She was particularly pleased that Luke was 'more animated than I have ever seen him'. She was impressed that the session 'wasn't just science but extends into other areas of the curriculum and therefore was a valuable use of time'. She was convinced of the value of recording children's comments in a floor-book and recognised the importance of this to assessment. She was still somewhat sceptical about organising such work whilst having responsibility for the whole class. Jill reassured her that the children can be trained to let a teacher focus attention on a small group and not interrupt. Overall, she concluded, 'I feel I and the children have gained from the work'. She agreed to try similar work with another group later in the week when she again had the support of the general assistant.

Jill's analysis of the day was also positive although she noted a concern about the type of questions Anna was asking. This had been discussed briefly during the analysis. Jill recognised that this issue needed addressing more generally and, at a staff meeting, introduced a discussion on the types of questions teachers ask. The general assistant also seemed to gain a great deal from the experience and Jill had evidence, a few weeks later, when she was in her class during SATs work, that the assistant was indeed valuing children's contributions during science activities.

As noted at the beginning of this case-study, the support described was the first stage of a continuing programme. Jill has since worked with Anna on a number of occasions and found evidence of changes to her classroom work. Anna is now regularly using floor-books and has put together several useful collections for scientific work. She is gradually gaining confidence and discussing her science work with some enthusiasm. Jill, during the first phase, had used a variety of modes of support. During the needs analysis there had been aspects of a zetetic mode which became the more predominant mode during later phases of the support. The collaborative planning involved Jill, (in hortative mode), in telling Anna about the use of collections and floor-books; she provided some of the collection of fabrics (provisionary mode) and during the first teaching session invited Anna to observe her own practice (role modelling mode); the analysis of her teaching and, later, Anna's, allowed further use of a zetetic mode. Jill thus successfully offered support to her less-confident colleague in a variety of ways.

Change in schools does not happen overnight. It is a slow, and a sometimes painful, process. However, a collaborative approach of the type described above can play a significant part in that process.

There are other models of collaborative work involving co-ordinators and colleagues which, in our experience, have proved successful. Co-ordinator and teachers can collaboratively plan work for groups which pairs of teachers implement in a team-teaching mode. The feed-back to their classes by each group of children can then provide a valuable opportunity for less confident colleagues to gain new perspectives on their classes and teaching, through activities that they and the co-ordinators have been implementing. Follow-up discussions and further collaborative planning for activities which the teachers can implement on their own are a development of this approach.

Another successful approach has involved co-ordinators planning a specific workshop or circus of activities, perhaps around a theme or children's book, which is set up in a hall or classroom. Other teachers can then visit the workshop with their classes, perhaps with parental help. The co-ordinator can be observed working with the class and can spend time talking to colleagues about the nature of the activities and the children's responses. Ideally, the whole school staff will get involved in planning such workshops and the planning stage will provide added opportunities for professional development. Such workshops can also be valuable for convincing parents of the benefits and nature of primary science.

The opportunities provided when students involved in initial teacher education are on school placements, can also be exploited by co-ordinators. In many areas it is common for teachers, students and college tutors to work collaboratively together in classrooms. This approach, often called IT-INSET, can provide benefits for all concerned, particularly when it is organised in a way that allows all three participants to be equal partners. The intention to make initial training more school-based offers increased opportunities for this kind of work.

8. Supporting change in classrooms

The zetetic mode, discussed briefly above, is one that we would wish to advocate since it most closely matches the approach to professional development introduced at the beginning of this chapter. The skilled co-ordinator can help colleagues engage in the process of action research. The skills needed in offering support to a reflective teacher are related to helping them:

- identify and explore a concern about their existing practice;
- focus on a specific aspect of that concern;
- consider new perspectives;
- set realistic goals;
- generate practical ways forward to meet those goals;
- plan precise action and decide what evidence should be collected to evaluate such action;
- implement the new approach and collect evidence;
- analyse evidence and evaluate;
- refine or revise the original concern.

In offering such support the co-ordinator needs numerous skills including clarifying, summarising, questioning and challenging, but, perhaps most importantly, the co-ordinator needs to listen (NCET, 1989). It should always be remembered that it is the individual teacher who is engaging in a process of personal change and the co-ordinator's role is to support them in that change. Change is often a painful process. Teachers, identifying their own professional needs, can see them as incompetencies of which they had previously been unaware. Individuals who are unaware of their incompetencies are happy in their ignorance and revealing concerns can lead to feelings of inadequacy and frustration. Such a step should only be taken if there is support available for teachers in addressing those concerns so that they will become consciously competent in those particular areas. In time, they may then be able to integrate new strategies and ways of working into their practice and become 'unconsciously' competent, by which is meant that the new way of working has become a natural part of their professional behaviour.

In summary, Michael Fullan (1982) offers a useful set of assumptions about change:

(1) Don't assume that your ideas about changes are the ones that ought to be implemented.
(2) Assume that individuals who are attempting to implement changes will continually need clarification about them in order to make sense.
(3) Assume that successful change will inevitably involve some conflict and disagreement.
(4) Assume that people will only change if there is pressure to do so, a supportive environment, and opportunities to share experiences with others in similar situations.
(5) Assume that it will take two or three years for significant change to take place.
(6) Don't assume that the change itself has been rejected if it fails to be implemented – there may be other factors which have contributed to the failure.
(7) Assume that it is impossible to bring about widespread change in a school: aim to increase the number of people affected.
(8) Assume that you need a knowledge of the factors which affect change and draw up a plan which takes account of them and the above assumptions.
(9) Don't assume that knowledge can be the sole basis for decisions. They will usually be based on a combination of knowledge, politics and intuition.
(10) Assume that change will be fraught with problems and new challenges.

9. Other opportunities for Professional Development

So far, this chapter has focused on school-based professional development and this is certainly the key area for most teachers. However, LEA and Higher Education institutions provide centre-based INSET opportunities for developing professional skills and knowledge and understanding in science. These vary from one-day courses organised by advisers or advisory teachers to year-long award-bearing courses in HE institutions. Such courses can provide a valuable stimulus for school-based changes, but there is evidence that many have limited impact back in school unless the school-based dimension is built into the course approach and structure. Our experience of INSET activities in primary science over the last few years has caused us to question the value of short sharp courses which do not have some built-in follow-up support. There seem to be a number of features which are characteristic of successful centre-based INSET activities. These include:

- making the intentions of the course explicit to prospective course members;
- identifying and addressing individual teachers' needs within the course;
- gaining the support of headteachers for school-based follow-up work by course members;
- encouraging schools to link course aims with Institutional Development Plans where possible;
- involving more than one teacher from a school in some aspects of the course;
- including specific and supported school-based tasks;
- encouraging teachers to engage in classroom-enquiries, focused upon their individual concerns and supported by other course members and tutors;
- providing opportunities to work collaboratively with fellow course members;
- recognising adult learning styles;
- ensuring that the teaching styles of tutors can be replicated by course members;
- facilitating post-course support, through local support groups or LEA networks.

We have attempted to build these features into our work on INSET courses over the last few years (Ritchie, 1989; 1991c; Ollerenshaw and Ritchie, 1990). Our most recent collaboration in this area has involved DES-approved 20-day science courses. The DES has funded a major initiative since 1989 to develop primary teachers' knowledge and understanding in the areas of science and mathematics. The approved course running at

Bath College of Higher Education for teachers from Avon and Wiltshire is based on our experience of a variety of modes of INSET provision. It is designed to be a centre-based course with built-in school-based elements to ensure the maximum impact in course members' classrooms and schools. Evaluative evidence collected for the first cohorts suggest it is being successful in meeting its aims of:

- improving primary teachers' knowledge and understanding of science;
- improving teachers' pedagogical skills in teaching science;
- encouraging course members to disseminate their change in practice to colleagues.

The course involves five cycles of four days (spread over a half-term) and each cycle has a content focus such as 'Forces' or 'Living things'. The first day and a half of each cycle involves workshops at the teachers' own level during which they engage in scientific exploration and investigation. These involve phases of orientation (for example, watching a video sequence of forces in everyday life); elicitation (producing a concept map of existing ideas about forces); restructuring (testing the effect of gravity of different objects); and review (discussing results and explanations). The tutors attempt to provide role-models that teachers can relate to their own practice. The afternoon of the second day is spent planning work for a group of children in the same content area. Day 3 is spent in one of the course members' classes. Each pair of teachers works with a small group, one teaching whilst the other observes and collects data. The first teaching session is usually an exploratory activity during which the teacher elicits the children's existing ideas. An analysis of this data during the second half of the morning is used to inform decisions about the afternoon session. The course members' roles are reversed and the children are encouraged to engage in more investigative work to challenge or develop the ideas they have. A second analysis is used to illuminate discussions about the nature of the children's learning.

There is a gap of several weeks during which the course members engage in their own classroom enquiries and work with their own children in the cycle's content area. The final centre-based day is used to review this work, deal with concerns the teachers have identified about their own knowledge and understanding and provide opportunities for them to apply any new understandings they have developed during the cycle.

There is evidence that teachers' own knowledge and understanding in an area of science can be developed through the identification and consideration of children's alternative ideas and their relationship with the teachers' own views and, indeed, the scientists' views which are offered by the tutors. The explicit use of a constructivist approach with the teachers has led to their adopting a similar approach to their own classroom work. For example, visits six months after the first course finished provided evidence of all the teachers in the sample eliciting their children's existing ideas more often than before the course and, significantly, basing decisions about activities upon that information.

10. Using Distance-learning Materials

Not all teachers can attend long courses and there are other ways in which their professional needs can be met. The current interest in improving primary teachers' background knowledge and understanding in science has led to a number of useful publications which are designed to be used independently by teachers. The NCC has commissioned two excellent publications on 'Forces' (NCC, 1992a) and 'Electricity' (NCC, 1992b) which provide a self-contained programme for teachers to use individually or, perhaps more profitably, in collaboration with colleagues. There is also an audio-tape on forces for those who prefer to listen rather than read. There is a clear constructivist view apparent in these materials.

The PSTS project, mentioned in Chapter 2, has produced packages of materials to address the range of alternative scientific ideas their original research with teachers revealed. At the present, packs covering Forces and Energy are available (PSTS, 1991a & b). These extensive materials claim to offer a constructivist approach but are extremely structured and provide limited opportunities for individuals genuinely to start from their own existing ideas. They do, however, offer some useful assistance for teachers who may find the constant use of analogies helpful. The Royal Society of Chemistry has also published a book, covering their interest area, that is free to schools. (Archer, 1991). The Open University publishes self-tutoring and tutored material to help primary teachers improve their own knowledge and understanding of science.

All these materials can be a means of supporting professional development in primary science teaching. However, there is a risk that the use of such material will encourage teachers to see the development of scientific knowledge and understanding as separate from the development of scientific processes and process skills. We have stated explicitly throughout this book that we regard them as inextricably linked, and this holds for the way in which children and adults develop knowledge and understanding. Consequently, we would encourage the use of these materials in the context of teachers' engaging in practical exploration and investigation based on their own questions. The materials will then become the means by which teachers gain access to more accepted scientific ideas to be tested alongside their own.

In the area of professional skills and knowledge and understanding there are other materials available. Some of these, such as the Science School Development Programme (Ollerenshaw, 1992b), offer a comprehensive and holistic package for whole-school use in supporting teachers' professional development. It is a flexible and comprehensive set of units designed to be used to meet the institutional and personal needs of primary teachers attempting to cope with the National Curriculum demands in science.

11. Conclusion

Professional development is an essential concern for all teachers, from those in their first year of teaching to experienced co-ordinators for science. All individuals have to take responsibility for their own programme of development, although at a time when teacher appraisal is pending this will inevitably become part of the dialogue between appraiser and appraisee. The best examples of appraisal have been shown to help individuals to identify their needs, set realistic targets to address them and provide the means by which those targets can be met – in fact, precisely as we advocate here. However, change in a teacher's practice cannot be imposed; it will be effective only if it is motivated by the individual's desire to change and where there is a commitment by the individual to effect change. Effective change requires strategies for professional development which give teachers ownership of their learning. We believe action research and opportunities to work collaboratively with fellow professionals are the keys to this. We hope the examples discussed in this chapter will encourage you to explore, within your own classroom and school, similar approaches, in order to improve the quality of the educational experience of your children.

Bibliography

Archer, D. (1991) *What's your reaction?* London: Royal Society of Chemistry

Assessment of Performance Unit (APU) (1983) *Science at Age 11.* London: DES

Assessment of Performance Unit (APU) (1984) *Science in Schools: Age 11.* London: DES

Assessment of Performance Unit (APU) (1989) Assessment Matters: No.2, 'Measurement in School Science', SEAC. London:HMSO

Ausubel, D. (1968) *Educational Psychology: A Cognitive View.* New York: Holt, Rinehart and Winston

Barnes, D. (1976) *From Communication to Curriculum.* Harmondsworth: Penguin

Barnes, D., Britton, J., Torbe, M., (1986) *Language, The Learner and the School*

Britton, V. (1972) *Language and Learning.* Harmondsworth: Pelican

Broadfoot, P. and Towler, L. (1992) 'Self-assessment in the Primary School,' *Educational Review;* Vol.44 No.2.

Carey, S. (1989) 'Cognitive Science and Science Education' in Murphy, P. and Moon, B. *Developments in Learning and Assessment.* Milton Keynes: Open University Press

Cavendish, S., Galton, M., Hargreaves, L. & Harlen, W. (1990) *Assessing Science in the Primary Classroom: Observing Activities.* London: Paul Chapman Publishing

CLIS (1984-91) *Children's Learning in Science Project Reports.* Leeds: Centre for the Study of Science and Mathematics Education

DES (1992a) *Science in the National Curriculum* (Revised). London: HMSO

DES (1992b) *Assessment, Recording and Reporting.* A Report by HMI on the second year, 1990-1991. London: HMSO

Driver, R. and Bell, B. (1985) 'Students' thinking and the learning of science: A constructivist view.' *School Science Review,* March '86 443-456

223

Driver, R. (1983) *The Pupil as Scientist*. Milton Keynes: Open University Press

Driver, R., Guesne, E. and Tiberghien, A. (1985) *Children's Ideas in Science*. Milton Keynes: Open University Press

Driver, R. and Erickson, G. (1983) 'Theories-in-Action: Some Theoretical and Empirical Issues of Students' Conceptual Frameworks in Science' in *Studies in Science Education* 10 pp. 37-60

Eason, P. (1985) *Making School-centred INSET Work*. Milton Keynes: Open University Press

Ebbutt, D. and Elliot, J. (1985) *Issues in Teaching for Understanding*. London: Longmans

Elliot, J. (1991) *Action Research for Educational Change*. Milton Keynes: Open University Press

Fairburn, D.J. (1988) 'New approaches to recording and reporting achievements' in Murphy, R. and Torrance, H. (eds) *The Changing Face of Educational Assessment*. Milton Keynes: Open University Press

Fullan, M. (1982) *The Meaning of Educational Change*. New York: Teachers College Press

Galton, M., Simon, B. and Croll, P. (1980) *Inside the Primary Classroom*. London: Routledge and Kegan Paul

Gilbert, C. and Watts, D.M. (1983) 'Concepts, Misconceptions and Alternative Conceptions: Changing Perspectives in Science Education' in *Studies in Science Education* 10 pp. 61-98

Gilbert, J.K., Watts, D.M. and Osbourne, R.J. (1985) 'Eliciting Students' Views Using Interviews About Instances Technique.' *Physics Education*, Vol.17 No.2 pp. 62-65

Guesne, E. (1978) 'Lumiere et vision des objets' in Delacote, G. (ed) *Physics Teaching in Schools*. London: Taylor and Francis

Harland, J. (1990) *The Work and Impact of Advisory Teachers*. Slough: NFER

Harlen, W. (1985) *Teaching and Learning in Primary Science*. London: Harper and Row

Harlen, W. (1992) *The Teaching of Science*. London: David Fulton

Hemsley, K et al. (1991) Information Technology Special. *Primary Science Review*, December, No. 20

Hewson, M. and Hamlyn, D. (1984) 'The Influence of Intellectual Environment on Conceptions of Heat' in *European Journal Science Ed.* 6 (3) pp. 245-262.

Hopkins, D. (1985) *A Teacher's Guide to Action Research*. Milton Keynes: Open University Press

Howard, S. (1992) 'Can you feel the force?' *Questions* February Vol. 4 No.5 pp. 18-19

Jelly, S. (1985) 'Helping children raise questions – and answering them' in Harlen, W.(ed) *Taking the Plunge*. London: Heinemann

Lewin, K. (1946) 'Action Research and Minority Problems' *in Journal of Social Issues* Vol. 2

Light, P., Sheldon, S. and Woodhead, M. (1991) *Learning How to Think*. Milton Keynes: Open University Press

McNiff, J. (1988) *Action Research: Principles and Practice*. London: Macmillan

Micros and Primary Education (MAPE) (1989) Primary Science: The Role of Information Technology. Microscope Special, Autumn

Mumby, S. (1989) *Assessing and Recording Achievements*. London: Blackwell

Muschamp, Y. (1992) 'Pupil Self Assessment', *PIPE* Issue No.8. Bristol: National Primary Centre (SW)

NCET (1989) *Working with Teachers*. Coventry: National Council for Educational Technology

NCC (1989) *Science: Non-statutory Guidance*. York. National Curriculum Council

NCC (1992a) *Forces*. York: National Curriculum Council

NCC (1992b) *Electricity*. York: National Curriculum Council

Novak, J.D. and Gowin, D.B. (1984) *Learning How to Learn*. Cambridge: Cambridge University Press

Ollerenshaw, C. (1989) 'Growing new ears' in *Questions* July No.9 pp. 8-9

Ollerenshaw, C. et al. (1991) *Constructive Teacher Assessment*. Bristol: National Primary Centre (SW)

Ollerenshaw, C. (1992a) 'Seeing is believing!' *in Junior Education* March 16 (3) pp. 24-25.

Ollerenshaw, C. (1992b) *School Development Programme: Science*. Bristol: Redland Centre, Bristol Polytechnic

Ollerenshaw, C. and Ritchie, R. (1990) 'The Advisory Teacher and Action Research,' in Petrie, P. (ed) *The Advisory Teacher – a Collection of Perspectives*. Hatfield: ASE

Osborne, R. and Freyberg, P. (1985) *Learning in Science: The Implications of Children's Science*. London: Heinemann

Parker-Rees, R., Thyer, J. and Ollerenshaw, C. (1991) Co-ordinator's Handbook in Ollerenshaw, C. et al. *Constructive Teacher Assessment*. Bristol: National Primary Centre (SW)

Piaget, J. (1929) *The Child's Conception of the World*. London: Routledge and Kegan Paul

Pollard, A. (1985) *The Social World of the Primary School*. London: Holt, Rinehart and Winston

Pollard, A. and Tann, S. (1987) *Reflective Teaching in the Primary School.* London: Cassell

Presst, B. (1980) *Problems with Words,* in ASE Language in Science Study Series No.16. Hatfield: Association for Science Education

PSTS (1988-91) *Primary School Teachers and Science Project Reports.* Oxford: University of Oxford

PSTS (1991a) *Primary School Teachers and Science Project: Understanding Forces.* Oxford: University of Oxford

PSTS (1991b) *Primary School Teachers and Science Project: Understanding Energy.* Oxford: University of Oxford

Rowland, S. (1984) *The Enquiring Classroom: an Introduction to Children's Learning.* Lewes: Falmer Press

Ritchie, R. (1989) 'Looking at Learning.' *Primary Science Review,* No.10. pp. 22-23

Ritchie, R. (1991a) *Profiling in Primary Schools.* London: Cassell

Ritchie, R. (1991b) 'IT's a Minibeast' in *Primary Science Review,* December No.20 pp. 12-15

Ritchie, R. (1991c) 'Generating Designs at Key Stages 1 and 2' *Design and Technology Teaching* Vol.23 pp. 132-134

Ritchie, R. (1992) 'Data Handling in Science at Key Stage 1' in Lodge, J. (ed) *Computer Data Handling in the Primary School.* London: David Fulton

Russell, T. and Harlen, W. (1990) *Assessing Science in the Primary Classroom: Practical Tasks.* London: Paul Chapman Publishing

Schiller, C. (1979) *In His Own Words.* London: A & C Black

SPACE (1990-92) Science Processes and Concept Exploration Project Reports. Liverpool: Liverpool University Press

Schilling, M., Harlen, W., Hargreaves, L. and Russell, T. (1990) *Assessing Science in the Primary Classroom: Written Tasks.* London: Paul Chapman Publishing

Schon, D. (1983) *The Reflective Practitioner.* London: Temple Smith

Scott, P. (1987) *A Constructivist View of Learning and Teaching in Science,* Centre for the Study of Science and Mathematics Education. Leeds: University of Leeds

Solomon, J. (1980) *Teaching Children in the Laboratory.* London: Croom-Helm

Stenhouse, L. (1975) *An Introduction to Curriculum Research and Development.* London: Heinemann

Task Group on Assessment and Testing (TGAT) (1987) A Report. London: DES

Tizard, B. and Hughes, M. (1984) *Young Children Learning.* London: Fontana

Toulmin, S. (1972) 'The Collective Use and Evolution of Concepts,' in *Human Understanding* Vol.1. Princeton: University of Princeton

Von Glasersfeld, E. (1989) 'Learning as a Constructive Activity' in Murphy, P. and Moon, B. (eds) *Developments in Learning and Assessment*. London: Hodder and Stoughton

Wellington, J. (1989) *Skills and Processes in Science Education: A Critical Analysis*. London: Methuen

Wells, G. (1986) *The Meaning Makers, Children Learning Language and Using Language to Learn*. London: Heinemann

Whitehead, J. and Foster, D. (1984) Action Research and Professional Development. CARN Bulletin, No.6 (Cambridge Institute of Education)

Whitehead, J. and Barrett, J. (1985) *Supporting Teachers in their Classroom Research*. Values in Education Group Paper. Bath: University of Bath